THE
ISLE OF DOGS
1066 ~ 1918
A BRIEF HISTORY
VOLUME I

AN ISLAND HISTORY TRUST
PUBLICATION
BY EVE HOSTETTLER

Eve Hostettler is the curator of the Island History Trust;
she has worked with the project since 1980

One of the mills on Millwall, from a water-colour painting, c1840

Foreword

The people who have really made this book possible are the hundreds of Islanders, and descendants of Islanders, who have given tape-recorded reminiscences, autobiographies, photographs and family histories to the archives of the Island History Trust during the twenty years of its existence. The Trust would also like to acknowledge the continuing and valuable support of Tower Hamlets Local Studies Archive in providing access to books and records; the Isle of Dogs Community Foundation and the National Lottery "Awards For All" Scheme for financial help in producing the book; and the Guildhall Library, the National Maritime Museum and the Museum of London (PLA Collection) for providing some of the photographs. Grateful thanks to all these institutions and also to Derek Chambers for his design work. Readers may like to know that unless otherwise stated, illustrations are taken from the Island History Trust Photograph Collection. All errors and omissions are the responsibility of the author.

This book is intended for the general reader and is an attempt to set the history of the Isle of Dogs in its context of national change over the centuries. It does not deal in any detail with the history of the West India and Millwall Docks, except in so far as they impact on the general development of the Island and the lives of Islanders, since this has been done elsewhere. A list of sources at the end of this book may be useful for further reading or research.

The second volume in this brief history of the Isle of Dogs, *Memory and Change in the 20th Century*, will follow, and will include a map and an index to both volumes.

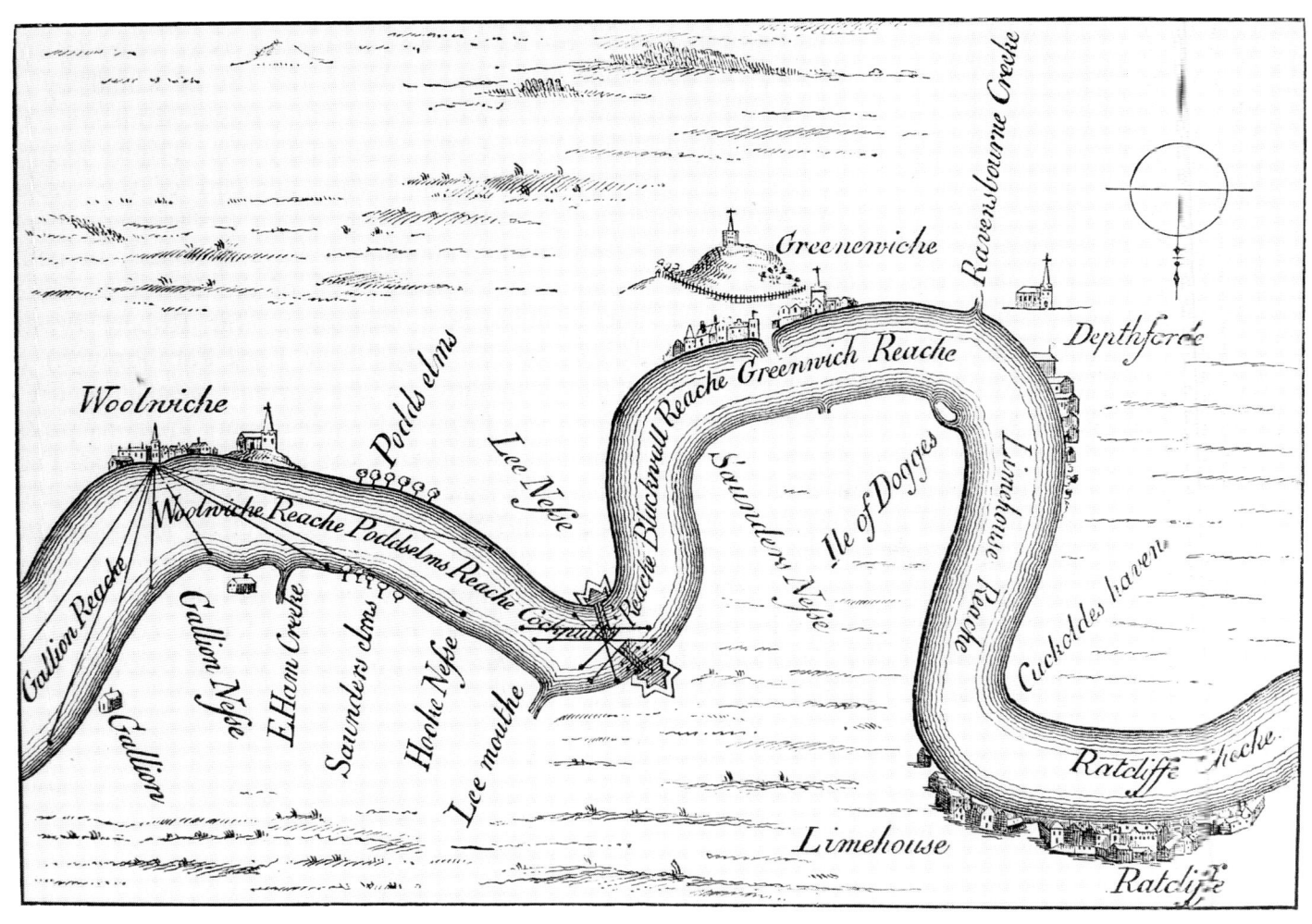

Copy of a map drawn up to indicate the defences of the Thames in 1588

Contents

From the Normans to Napoleon

1. Pre-industrial times- 1066 to 1800   6

The First Industrial Phase - 1800 to the 1860s

2. Introduction 22

3. Ship-building on the Isle of Dogs 24

4. Roads, Railways, Homes 32

5. All Kinds of People 39

6. Aspects of Everyday Life 44

The Second Industrial Phase - 1860s to 1914

7. Introduction 53

8. The Industrial Island 55

9. Transport and Buildings 65

10. Island People 76

11. Working Life 86

12. Domestic Life 96

13. Social Life and Leisure 104

The First World War 1914-1918

14. One Soldier's War 113

From the Normans to Napoleon

1. Pre-industrial times - 1066 to 1800

The original name of the Isle of Dogs was Stepney Marsh. There was a small island in the Thames, just off the south-west quadrant of the Marsh, marked on maps of the Tudor period as "Ile of Dogges". The reason for the name is lost to us. Over time, the island disappeared. The name remained and gradually became attached to the Marsh, giving rise to a rich variety of interpretations as to its meaning and its origins.

"Stepney" is more easily traced and comes from "Stebunhithe" a word of Saxon origin meaning "Stephen's Harbour". The name "Stepney" came to be applied to the area east of London along the bank of the Thames as far as the River Lea and north as far as Hackney.

From the Tower of London in the west to Blackwall in the east runs a low cliff or shelf of gravel. South of the cliff towards the river the land is naturally marshy and subject to flooding. Immediately to the east of the Tower this low-lying land formed Wapping Marsh. Further east, in the loop of the river between Limehouse and Blackwall, and opposite Greenwich on the south bank, lay Stepney Marsh. It has also been called Poplar Marsh, and Wet Marsh.

There may have been people living in the marshy part of Stepney we now call the Isle of Dogs in Roman or even in pre-Roman times, but if so, no definite evidence of their presence has been found, unless we include the discovery of one third-century Roman coin which could have been dropped at any time before it came to light in 1844.

It is thought that the embankment wall of earth, wood and stones was constructed in early medieval times. This wall, which had to be frequently repaired and strengthened, kept out the river Thames at high tide and allowed the enclosed land to be cultivated. According to medieval wills and other legal documents, Stepney Marsh was owned by religious bodies and wealthy individuals.

From the 15th century onwards, land everywhere passed out of Church ownership into private hands and whilst agriculture remained the chief occupation on Stepney Marsh, the nearby villages of Blackwall, Limehouse and Poplar began to develop their maritime and trading character.

We know that in the second half of the 12th century (that is, following the Norman invasion and settlement) William of Pontefract had an estate on Stepney Marsh of about 80 acres and including a windmill. There was a chapel here too. (The chapel and manor house stood close by the future site of Millwall Dock Graving Dock in what is now Clipper Quay estate. "Chapel House Street" was built nearby in 1920).

Pontefract Manor may have been land and a community appropriated by the new king from its previous Saxon owners and given to William, one of his soldiers or henchmen, as a reward for services. Or, William of Pontefract, who would have brought with him his own retainers and servants, may have founded a new community here. (It seems to have passed to his descendants, as Richard de Pontefract still held land in Stepney in the 14th century). Any existing Saxons would have had to move off or settle down with their new master. This latter option might not have been too difficult since although Norman rule brought many changes, the Saxon system of landholding and cultivation was continued with little alteration.

Threshing, 11th Century

From medieval books of husbandry and other records we can work out what the Manor of Pontefract was like and how life was lived there.

The Manor house was moated for defensive purposes and built, like the chapel, at least partly of stone. If it was anything like a manor house at Shadwell of the same period, it had a hall, or large main room, cellar, buttery, pantry and living room. Close to the Pontefract Manor house and chapel were smaller dwellings of wattle and thatch, shared between humans and animals. Near at hand were strip fields for corn and pulses (beans and peas), common lands for grazing hogs, cattle, sheep and the oxen who drew the plough, copses of hazel or willow cultivated for firewood and building materials, reed beds in which wild fowl nested and which were harvested for thatch, and nets in the river for fish.

Any medieval manor had to be largely self-sufficient in food, fuel and building materials. The Lord of the Manor had his own holding or demesne, which was cultivated for him by the people who owed him feudal services - usually the families who lived and farmed communally nearby. He also owned the mill, and his tenants had to pay to use it. The grinding of corn by hand had been suppressed by this time in order to add to the Lord's revenue. Since flour was a staple food, the miller occupied a position of privilege and power in the community, which explains why he is so often depicted as a villain in medieval story and song. The Lord's tenants might also have to pay to use his baking oven (ovens in their own fragile homes being too dangerous and too expensive), and may have had to pay for whatever other privileges the Lord chose - the right to gather firewood being one.

Aside from the land owned by Pontefract manor, until the 16th century large acreages of the marsh were owned at various periods by the Abbey of St. Mary of Graces and by the Bishop of London. These lands were farmed to supply the Abbey with food, or sub-let by the Bishop to tenant farmers in return for money rent or produce. The Abbey had 95 acres of marsh and 135 acres of arable land, yielding valuable supplies of corn, animal fodder and fish.

The early medieval community on Stepney Marsh was organised on feudal lines and depended for its survival on farming and fishing. The period after harvest was when the farming year began with the ploughing of the wheat field, after which winter wheat and rye would be sown broadcast by hand. Hens, sheep and pigs were fed on the stubble of the remaining two fields. After ploughing the cattle were brought in for the winter, and those that could not be kept through the winter (because of a shortage of animal feed) would be slaughtered and the carcasses salted or smoked. Threshing was done in winter, peas and beans as well as corn being threshed and the wheat winnowed by hand. Malted barley was used for brewing, which was done in the home.

When winter was over the second field was ploughed for the sowing of peas, beans, vetches, oats and barley. Tenants who were not occupied

Medieval haymakers

in ploughing, sowing or animal husbandry had work found for them in the garden and orchards of the manor, where apples, pears and quinces, leeks, onions, mustard, herbs and peas were grown; there was also fishing, dairy work, the making of clothes and household linens, repairs to buildings, fences and boats to be done. Many tasks were undertaken communally.

Men, women and children all worked as the season required and as custom decreed. Local customs, feudal duties and obligations varied according to the nature and needs of the area. For example, it was the custom, first revealed in the records in 1334 but said to have been established "at a time unknown" for a lord of the manor in Stepney to appoint wall reeves to inspect the river walls and warn tenants when repairs were needed. In the mid-14th century the labour services on the 80 acres of arable land in Pontefract Manor consisted of "reaping the corn that grew there".

The inhabitants of Stepney Marsh in medieval times lived closer to nature, and were much more vulnerable to its unpredictable forces, than ourselves.

They rose at or before sunrise and went to

sleep when it grew dark. They wore homespun woollen clothing and handmade leather footwear; they rarely washed and were subject to infectious diseases and other illnesses virtually eliminated in our society. They used handmade tools and simple mechanical devices. They knew how to handle horses and use herbs for medicine, they could kill and skin a hog and turn every part of it into something edible or useful. They were Christians who also held firmly to many beliefs and superstitions not taught by the church.

Their social order was one of duty and obligation to give work or service to those next above them in the hierarchy, who in turn owed them a duty of protection, all too often translated into exploitation. There were small communities similar to this one all over England and Europe between the 10th and 14th centuries, the time of the Crusades, of small kingdoms struggling to defend and extend their territories, of barons seeking to assert their rights in relation to kings, of walled cities, pitched battles, plague and famine. Spain was still a largely Muslim country, France a collection of dukedoms or princely states, and England was being painfully unified into one kingdom under the Norman kings and their successors.

We can surmise that the lives of the people of Stebunheath Marsh were bound up in the demands of daily survival and that scant news reached them from the outside world, or reached them only long after the event. There is no evidence that the Black Death of the early 14th century, or the Peasants Revolt of 1381, had any impact upon the people of the Marsh. We do know, though, that Wat Tyler's army met the King and his men at Mile End and that enormous quantities of extra food must have been needed for these visitors. Part of Wat Tyler's peasant army camped at Blackheath in 1381 - how would they have reached Mile End? Did some cross the river by ferry to Stepney Marsh in order to further their campaign for an end to serfdom and poverty?

From the Marsh, London was a smokey blur to the west, a place of power, wealth, exotic goods and merchants and sailors from distant lands. The city had been an important port since Roman times, and the small rounded ships which sailed to and fro along the Thames past the Marsh carried imports of wines, silks, salt and spices from Europe and the Mediterranean lands, to be exchanged for exports of grain, raw wool and metal goods in a pattern of commerce frequently checked by conflict but always ready

to resume and grow again.

Records indicate the continued existence of a farming community on the Marsh during the 14th and 15th centuries although the original manor house of Pontefract was in ruins by 1362. The mill had also fallen into dis-use. The chapel, which may have been rebuilt and was by now dedicated to St. Mary, survived for another hundred years. It is believed to have been a chapel of ease connected to St. Dunstan's Church in Stepney. The chapel was supported by members of its congregation, who left money for specific purposes. The chaplain was named as Stephen, in 1382 and 1392, John, in 1394 (not everyone had surnames), John Dancastell in 1397 (he died in 1407) and Thomas Muncton in 1432 and 1438. One woman, Agnes Baget, when she died in 1415, left eightpence for the upkeep of the West Window. An exceptionally detailed will was that of John Broom who died in 1402.

14th century ships

He left three shillings and fourpence to the image of Our Lady in the marsh chapel, one shilling and eightpence to John, the parochial chaplain and sixpence to John the clerk at the same chapel. He left four mares, four cows and 22 sheep to his sons and friends, evidence of stock-raising on the marsh.

Fishmongers and fishermen lived in Poplar and on the Marsh by the end of the 14th and beginning of the 15th century, and quite probably for centuries before they appear in the records. Like all trades in medieval times, fishing was strictly controlled. Orders, issued by the Mayor of London as Admiral of the Thames, governed the size and positioning of nets and traps; these rules were designed to prevent over-fishing and keep the river clear for shipping. Disputes sometimes led to legal action and the names of some local fishermen appear in the resulting records. There was Solomon Prat of

Poplar, John Thresher of Poplar, Roger Sket and Roger Gromet of Poplar, the last two named describing themselves as "of the marsh". They fished locally to the east of Stebunheath Marsh, probably for sale in the immediate area. Fishing did not develop as a major source of income here, as it did at Barking, because of the rise of alternative employment in shipping and seafaring. However there were lone fishermen who went further afield, like Elys Sharp who was robbed whilst on his way to Leigh on Sea to sell fish, and Thomas Warner of Poplar who may have sailed with the Barking boats; his will indicated that he owned a decked boat suitable for estuary fishing.

Medieval historian Kevin McDonnel points to the evidence of the medieval wills as an

Remains of the old Chapel in 1857

expression of community spirit and local loyalty. He suggests that people were proud to be associated with Poplar (including the marsh) as an area where there was on the one hand the stability provided by a large ecclesiastical manor (the Abbey of Graces) and on the other a turning towards the Thames, with fishing and the beginning of shipbuilding at Limehouse and Ratcliffe, giving the place a distinctive character which differentiated it from other inland parts of Stepney. This local pride was expressed in financial support for the chapel and by extension for the community which used it.

To leave money to the church was also an act of piety, an aid to salvation and helped to ensure respect for one's memory.

Farming on Stebunheath Marsh suffered a setback when due to the neglect of the embankment wall, the marsh was flooded in 1449. Most historians of the period agree that the hamlet of Pontefract manor fell into decline

at this time, and there is no further evidence of corn-growing after that date. The rising population of the capital however, created an ever-expanding market for food and made agriculture profitable, especially for landowners. The Bishop of London and his tenants invested large sums in reclaiming the flooded lands during the 15th and early 16th centuries. They had only limited success, but whenever possible, the marshy pastures were used for holding and fattening cattle brought to London for slaughter. Benet Jackson was one London butcher who had marsh ground in Poplar Marsh and Stepney Marsh. The slaughter of cattle was only permitted in two places - Stepney and Knightsbridge - so pasture in Stepney would be convenient for a butcher to keep surplus stock.

The 13th and 14th centuries had seen the great expansion of Britain's production of raw wool and its export to Europe, founding many fortunes in the process. London's foreign trade was in much more than wool, for it included exports of corn, fat cattle, hides and herrings; its imports were fine cloth from Flanders, wine from Gascony, Spain and the Rhineland, furs from Scandanavia, Toledo blades from Spain, Baltic timber, German armour, spices, gold and jewels from Venice and Asia. Hand in hand, the expansion of individual private enterprise and general economic growth broke the bonds that held feudal society together and from the 15th century onwards, signs of an emerging merchant capital society were everywhere apparent in England. London was expanding and so were all the villages adjacent to the Marsh, including Deptford and Greenwich across the river.

Changes in landownership were part of this general change and helped to stimulate growth. East London historian Alan Palmer points to the vast estates belonging to the Church to the east of the City of London and says: "As soon as the Church estates went up for sale in the middle of the 16th century, the eastern approaches to London experienced the greatest land revolution they had as yet known. Trades and crafts flourished outside the monopolistic grasp of the early livery companies". The entire Manor of Stepney, which had belonged to the Bishop of London, was surrendered to the king in 1551 and granted to Thomas, Lord Wentworth. Everywhere this movement of church lands into the hands of laymen opened the doors for commercial development.

Kevin McDonnell paints a picture of Limehouse, Ratcliffe, Poplar and Blackwall by the 16th century as riverside villages with a strong maritime connection and a mixed population, still retaining some of their rural character, especially on the marshes.

At Ratcliffe in the late 14th century and in Limehouse by the early 15th century a base for fitting out and victualling ships had developed with associated trades and suppliers and "all kinds and conditions of men who earned their living from the ship-building industry and who manned the ships which were built there or which lay at anchor close by.'" Returning sailors brought back tales of "Barbareye" of "Africks monsters and Guianaes rarities".

The population of the Tower hamlets included Londoners moving to the eastern suburbs and migrants from other parts of England, from Lincolnshire, Devon, Kent, Essex, Lancashire, Suffolk, Wales, Scotland and Ireland. There were also many "aliens", immigrants from Holland, France and Germany.

McDonnell describes "the slow conquest of the fields by dwelling houses, warehouses and workplaces". Already by the 15th century a road, called in later years, The Highway, stretched from St.Katherines near the Tower to Ratcliffe and on to Limehouse until it became Poplar High Street. It ran all along a gravel terrace to the north of the marshy riverside ground. Some fine homes were built for the rich in the riverside villages, with beautiful gardens, including one in which, in 1549, 2,800 rose bushes were planted as well as fruit trees and herbs.

At this time Poplar was still a pleasantly wooded district. William Marrowe was a grocer and Lord Mayor of London from 1455-56. In order to pay for repairs to his London properties, he directed that his wood in Essex and Middlesex was to be sold with the exception of such timber, the removal of which would disfigure "my place in Poplar." During the reign of Henry VIII seven loads of elm were carried from Poplar to one of the King's manors.

At Blackwall the *Mary Rose* was fitted out in 1515-1516 and the King's men were lodged in Poplar while they worked. In 1549-50 hundreds of oxen were pastured on Stebunheath Marsh and then slain, their meat salted and barrelled for an expedition against the French. In the reign of Henry VIII goods were unloaded at Blackwall and the King's ships lay at Limehouse. Inhabitants of Poplar and Stebunheath Marsh were involved in maritime partnerships. In 1505 John Stevynson, mariner, of Poplar, had a share in the ship "Peter of London"; he also owned

houses, tenements and gardens in Poplar as well as a lease of five acres of land in Poplar Marsh.

The first evidence of a direct relationship between Greenwich and Stepney Marsh is the ferry service which appeared in the records in 1450, when it was mentioned in the will of Elizabeth Holden of Durham. It must have existed before that for it to become her property. It was in 1450 that Jack Cade's "Men of Kent", a broad-based popular army many thousands strong seeking political change, camped at Blackheath before moving on to quarter at Southwark. They hoped to persuade the King to make government more democratic. London merchants were initially friendly to them but on reflection blockaded London Bridge (at that time the only bridge). Other ways of crossing the river, perhaps through Stepney Marsh, may have been used.

It was at this time, in the middle of the 15th century, that Humphrey, Duke of Gloucester, created a park and mansion at Greenwich. He also built a tower, which became the site of the first Royal Observatory in the late 17th century. Duke Humphrey's property came into the hands of the Crown, and was used a great deal by successive monarchs. In the reign of Henry VIII sumptuous banquets, revels and jousts were held at Greenwich, and Queen Elizabeth I made it her summer residence. The growth of

Queen Elizabeth I

East of London Bridge in 1647

Greenwich may have stimulated traffic between the north and south banks of the river at this point.

As England evolved into a maritime trading nation and sought out new sources of raw materials and new markets for manufactured goods, the pressure intensified to extend the boundaries of the known world or to gain control of lands newly discovered. There were oceans and continents still to be charted and much still to learn about how to navigate the globe successfully. Competition for the rich rewards to be reaped from successful discovery and conquest led to intense rivalry between the European powers. The ocean voyages and the naval battles, piracy and skirmishes increased the demand for ships and sailors.

Expeditions sailed from London, along Limehouse Reach and Greenwich Reach, past anyone watching from the banks of Stebunheath Marsh, to vie with Holland, Spain and France for the lucrative trade of Central and South America, the East and West Indies, Africa, Ceylon and India.

To handle the growing cargoes flowing in and out of the port of London, the Legal Quays were built on the north bank of the Thames between London Bridge and the Tower early in the reign of Elizabeth. All dutiable goods had to be landed here, in order to safeguard the revenues of the Crown.

In 1580 Sir Francis Drake was knighted by Queen Elizabeth on the deck of the *Golden Hind* as it lay off Deptford, and a few years later the Queen sailed down the river to address her troops at Tilbury while the Spanish Armada was in the Channel. A map of the defences of the Thames, drawn up at this time, is one of the earliest known records of the original "Ile of Dogges".

By the end of the 16th century Ratcliffe and Blackwall were points of departure for expeditions of all kinds. The first trading fleet of the East India Company set sail from Woolwich in 1601 and in 1612 the Company established its base at Blackwall, leading to the further development of Poplar High Street with its taverns, dwelling houses and company chapel. Between 1628 and 1640, 20,000 Puritans, believing England was about to revert to Catholicism under the Stuart kings, set sail for New England, some of them departing from the quaysides of Ratcliffe and Blackwall. This movement created further cross-Atlantic connections. The expansion of an international trading network fostered the development of banking, insurance and shipbuilding in the two great European cities of London and Amsterdam and augmented the wealth of their merchants.

London's population in the 16th and 17th centuries grew from under 50,000 in 1509 to something less than half a million at the time of the Great Fire of London in 1666, creating an expansion in the internal market for food, particularly meat and grain. This expansion made agricultural land increasingly profitable for its owners and explains the efforts made to keep the Marsh secure for pasture by carrying out drainage works and repairing the embankment when it was breached. There was still a small farming community on the site of the old Pontefract Manor, though the chapel had fallen into disuse. A new house had been built. It was gabled, with a hipped red-tiled roof, suitable for the country residence of a person of wealth and high social status. In the 16th century it belonged to Thomas Knight, citizen and brewer of London, and in the following century it was part of Sir John Yate's estate. Near to the house stood barns and tenements.

An observer of the time described ways of earning a living in those parts of Middlesex which lay close to the capital, also giving an idea of the food which was eaten:

"...of such as inhabite near the Thames, they live either by the bardge, by the wherrye or ferrye, by the sculler or by fishinge, all of which live well and plentifullye, and in decent and honest sort releve their famelyes. Such as live in the body of the Shire...are men of husbandrye and they wholly dedicate themselves to the manuringe of their lande...the wyfe twice or thryce a weeke conveyethe to London mylke, butter, cheese, apples, peares, frumentye, hens, chickens, egges, baken and a thousand other country drugges which good huswifes can frame and find to get a pennye. And this yeldeth them a large comfort and reliefe...Another sort of husbandman...who havinge great feedinges for cattle and good breede for younge, often use Smithfelde and other lyke places with fatt cattle, wher also they store themselves with leane...Ther are also that live by carriage for other men and to that ende they keepe cartes and carriages, carry meale, milke and manie other thinges to London...".

The people who lived on Stebunheath Marsh were part of a very different society from the England of the 11th century and the feudal holding of William of Pontefract.

The intervening centuries had seen the emergence of a recognisably modern Europe with its nation states, its cathedral cities, its universities, commerce and its democratic forms of government, if only in embryonic forms. Religious and political struggles, new discoveries about the natural world, had resulted in an age of relative freedom of individual thought and action, a flowering of science, the arts and literature, including the great classics of the English language. Chaucer himself had lived and worked in the port of London in the 14th century and two hundred years later, Shakespeare's plays were performed in the capital to audiences which included both rich traders and poor seamen.

The feudal order had given way to a society concerned with manufacture and trade rather than with small-scale warfare. It was a fairer and a freer society than it had been, but it remained harsh and inhumane by our standards. Life was precarious and subject to extremes of poverty and injustice. The break up of the old monastic

Buy my Dish of great Eels.

Eel Seller, 1688

estates and the disintegration of feudal society had resulted in a movement of people out of the countryside towards the towns and the capital. There was not enough work for everyone and one of the great social problems of the 16th century was the army of the dispossessed, wandering the country or the streets of the capital, finding work when they could and begging for food when they could not.

In earlier times the giving of alms to beggars had been an acceptable act of Christian charity. Now it had become an unwelcome burden. The government's response to this situation was to introduce harsh penal laws so that, for example, in 1536 the law stated that "sturdy vagabonds" should have their ears cut off and in 1572 unlicensed beggars were to be flogged and branded

It is perhaps unlikely that many such "sturdy vagabonds" found their way to the sparsely inhabited and relatively inhospitable, windswept pastures of Stepney Marsh. People living on Stepney Marsh and the nearby villages at this time may have been descendants of earlier inhabitants. They may have been more recent arrivals from anywhere in the British Isles on one of the many ships which sailed up the Thames from other coastal towns and villages bringing fish, coal and grain to the capital. They may have arrived as families of drovers, deciding to settle near the capital rather than return to the broad fields of East Anglia.

Whoever they were, their existence was extremely hard and insecure by our standards, their clothes homespun, their tools hand-made. Travel was slow and costly. Hygiene was poor, infectious illnesses and high infant mortality were accepted as inevitable; traditional beliefs and superstitions still held sway alongside an increasingly rational Christianity. On the other hand they enjoyed fairs and travelling players, and attended Sunday service at St.Dunstan's or the East India Company chapel in Poplar High Street or at open-air meetings of Dissenting preachers at Mile End. Much of their knowledge and opinion of the rest of the world was gleaned from the tales of itinerant players, returning sailors, chance encounters with outsiders, and from the Sunday sermon, since there were few newspapers. News of the Civil War, the Restoration and the new powers of Parliament, would have reached them in this way.

Amongst the travellers who passed over the Marsh, and who might be engaged in conversation, the most famous was the diarist and Secretary to the Admiralty, Samuel Pepys. The ferry to Greenwich has been referred to already, and was known by the 16th century as Potter's Ferry, plying between the Isle of Dogs and Greenwich. There was also a ferry to Deptford from a point on the Island where the present Deptford Ferry Road, now a tiny cul-de-sac, met the river bank. Both ferries could be reached either along the top of the embankment from Limehouse or Blackwall, or from Harrow Lane in Poplar High Street, southwards by following East Ferry Road (its modern name) through the fields. Pepys was referring to the ferry to Deptford when he wrote of crossing the river as a foot passenger but being unable to get his coach over due to low water. He was on his way to a wedding, on July 31st, 1665 (a year before the Great Fire of London):

"Up and very betimes by six o'clock at Deptford and there I find Sir George Carteret and my lady ready to go; I being in my new coloured silk suit and coat trimmed with gold buttons and gold broad lace round my hands, very rich and fine. By water to the Ferry, where when we come no coach there; and tide of ebb, so far spent as the horse boat could not get off on the other side the river to bring away the coach. So we were fain to stay there, in the unlucky Isle of Doggs, in a chill place, the morning cool and wind fresh, above two, if not three hours, to our great discontent."

Pepys and his companions were forced to send the licence and wedding ring on ahead by horse whilst they waited for a coach and six, and when it came, drive as fast as they might, they still missed the ceremony, though not the celebrations which followed.

After London had been rebuilt in the years following the Great Fire of 1666, its population continued to increase, swollen by migrants from other parts of the British Isles as well as by slight increases in life expectancy brought about by improvements in diet. The capital's population of around half a million in 1666 had risen to 675,000 by 1700. Food production was rising in response to this expanding market; drainage schemes had brought new land into production, stronger ploughs, pulled by horses, were in use and the scythe had begun to replace the sickle at the harvest - small but significant changes.

In 1680, 200,000 quarters of corn were imported annually into the capital. By 1710 the annual amount was double that figure. This expansion brought new industry and population to Stepney Marsh.

For centuries much of the corn coming into London had been unloaded at the mills on the river Lea at Stratford, to be ground into flour. The rapid increase in the quantity of grain to be milled made the construction of new windmills a profitable undertaking and the mills which gave Mill Wall its name, a total of twelve in all, were built on the western embankment of Stepney Marsh between 1679 and 1740, five of them in the 1690s.

Several of the new Millwall mills were built by Rotherhithe millers. Milling could be a variable occupation, depending on the quality of

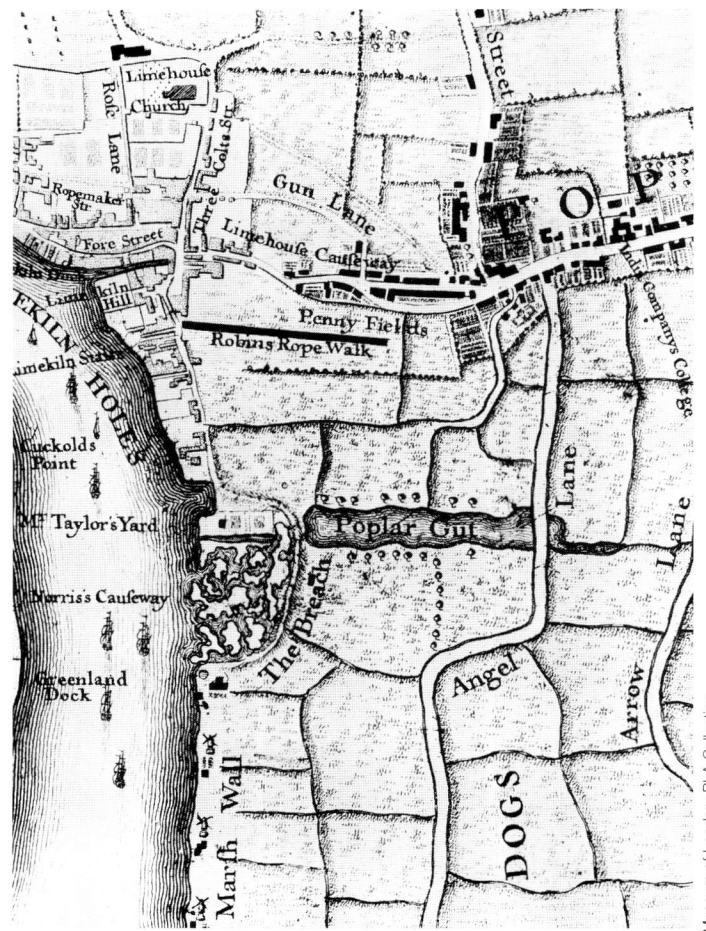

Section of John Rocque's Map of 1746

the harvest, the efficiency of transport and the state of the wind. Combining corn-milling with related activities made sound sense and others who had an interest in the mills at various times over the next hundred years included brewers, bakers, corn chandlers and biscuit makers, with businesses in Limehouse, Shadwell and Barking.

The mills on the marsh wall were in operation for most of the 18th century, in some cases being converted to crushing oil-seed by the end of that time. Some of the mill buildings were extensive, including granaries and a bakehouse, as well as cellars and cottage homes. Thus one of the first industries on the Isle of Dogs was flour milling, which brought with it increased activity and more people and population - barges loading and unloading at the wharves, millers, mill workers and their families living in the mill cottages, communications to and fro across the river and on foot or by horse along the riverside to the west.

The mills and their owners appear from time to time in legal records. The lease of a mill by Anne Price and Elizabeth Coates of Wapping, "the windmill called the seventh mill or Chinner's on Poplar Marshland or wall facing the Thames" to lighterman John Mitchell, for

twelve pounds per annum, is one such reference dated 1740. A more unusual reference appears in *The Anatomy of the Human Body* (1756), describing an accident in 1737 in which Samuel Wood, miller, had his arm torn off by mill machinery. The wound healed of its own accord with only a simple dressing. He was working in a mill on the Isle of Dogs at the time of his accident.

During the 18th century the pastures of the Marsh were in constant use for fattening cattle and sheep. That the drainage schemes of earlier times were not entirely effective can be judged from Gascoigne's note in his Survey of 1703, referring to "the Old Breach, or Forland now a place to lay timber" on the Marsh and from the fact that an inland lake, known as Poplar Gut, disappeared only when the West India Docks were built in 1800.

There were still hundred acres of pasture which were not permanently under water, and there are several eighteenth-century references to the animals fattened for sale on the Marsh. Strype, in 1720, wrote that oxen fed on the Marsh had been known to sell for thirty-four pounds each and that a Club at Blackwall was supplied with "a legge of mutton every week throughout the year, weighing not less than 28 pounds. Such legges of mutton to be cut from sheep fed on the Isle of Dogs marshes." Thomas Baker, a grazier of considerable standing on the Marsh, was known to have raised there: "one of the fattest head of cattle to have been seen in the Market during the whole year." In the 1770s another writer, Maitland, described "the Isle of Dogs, or Poplar Marsh" as being "a spot of ground of such fertility and excellence of grass, that it not only raises the largest cattle, but it is

A City Feast, 1770

likewise the great restorative of all distempered beasts." These special qualities were attributed by Middleton (1798) to the Island being divided by ditches which emptied themselves into the Thames at low water, keeping the soil fresh and light. Mr Mellish, owner of one of the largest areas of grazing on the Marsh, made a fortune by turning lean cattle on to these pastures and sending them on to Smithfield market, where high prices were maintained. He also profited from supplying the Navy during the Napoleonic Wars. Middleton claimed: "It is perhaps the richest grass in the county (of Middlesex)."

These comments on the size of animals reflect a revolution in agricultural practice on a national scale. The enclosure movement of the 18th century, particularly active between 1750 and 1780, had continued the process begun in earlier times, creating the countryside of England in its familiar form of scattered farm houses set amidst fields surrounded by hedges. With animals under their control, instead of grazing on the common land, modernising farmers could experiment with breeding to produce the animals which would bring in better profits - plump, fleecy sheep and fat cattle, instead of the scrawny creatures which had previously made up the flocks and herds fed on the common pastures of each village and hamlet. Increased production of hay and the use of turnips for fodder, allowed more and fatter animals to be kept over the winter.

Between 1710 and 1795 the average weight of calves sold at Smithfield increased from 50 pounds to 150 pounds, that of sheep from 38 pounds to 80 pounds. This included plump stock from the marshy pastures of the Isle of Dogs where a number of butchers and graziers like William Mellish and Thomas Baker owned or leased pasture land. These men employed others to manage their flocks, and to keep drains, fences and gates in good repair. People so employed lived either on the Marsh itself, in the former chapel, now a farm house, or nearby cottages, or they may have walked to work from Poplar or Limehouse.

In the 18th century Stebunheath Marsh (or the Isle of Dogs as it had by then begun to be more generally known) was still sparsely inhabited, but the neighbouring villages of Limehouse, Poplar and Blackwall had grown into busy communities as a result of the rapid growth of London and the eastward spread of industry and commerce. Closer to the City at Wapping there was "a labyrinth of rope-walks, breweries, small founderies, anchor forges, docks, sugar boilers, oil, colour and soap works and boat-builders yards...(amongst the)... irregularly-built homes and taverns for artisans, sailors, coal-heavers and other waterside workers..." In the fresher air of Limehouse at this time it was said that: "...several descriptions of naval artificers reside within it, where houses are frequently decorated with masts and flags, waving through the trees and interspersed among larger mansions of opulent merchants."

At Greenwich a new palace, started in the time of Charles II but unfinished, had become part of the Royal Naval Hospital, completed to a design by Sir Christopher Wren and opened to disabled seamen in 1705. The park, enlarged under Charles II, was the site of the popular Greenwich Fairs, held from Monday to Wednesday in Easter and Whitsun weeks. Originally established, like all medieval fairs, as a centre for trade and commerce, the fairs rapidly became occasions of popular amusement. They were, a 19th century observer remarked: "a vagabond resort and a scene of low frolic", or from another point of view, just the place to enjoy music, competitive sports, dancing and drinking with friends.

For anyone living on the Isle of Dogs, the way to the Greenwich Fair would have been by ferry. In 1762 the right to operate Potter's Ferry was granted to certain watermen at Greenwich who were permitted to carry: "men, horses, beasts and all other cattle and carriages whatsoever" across the river. This ferry operated from the river bank close to where the *Ferry House* pub stood at the end of the road through the Marsh from Poplar (now Ferry Street).

For people living in Limehouse, Poplar and

Mary Evans Picture Library

Preparing a Bull for Smithfield Show

Blackwall, the embankment walls of the Isle of Dogs offered a pleasant stroll on a fine day, past grazing animals, the windmills, the reed beds and copses of willow, with an ever-changing view of the shipping in the river and the vista of fine buildings at Greenwich with its green hills and woods beyond to please the eye. In the 18th century this outing naturally included a dinner, possibly of the famous whitebait. The leisurely lifestyle enjoyed by the well-off is suggested here:

"We finished our walk and dined at a small house called The Folly, on the water's edge almost opposite the splendid hospital at Greenwich, where we sat for some hours, enjoying the delicious view of the river and the moving picture of a succession of shipping perpetually passing and repassing."

The *Folly House* tavern was sited near the modern Folly Wall. If the gibbet with its gruesome cargo of the skeletons of former pirates stood on the south bank in Blackwall Reach, it would have been visible from that point on a clear day. If so, it was a reassuring expression of law and order for the passers-by, hardened as they undoubtedly were by public floggings and hangings. The practice of displaying the corpses of executed pirates on the banks of the Thames was adopted in 1700, apparently on the suggestion of William III. The gibbet was taken down in 1827, when a contemporary sketch showed the skeletons lying on the ground alongside the dismantled structure.

The existence of Folly House, the nearby Roult's shipyard, and of the Mast House erected in the same period near the site of the original "Ile of Dogges" (near the modern Mast House Terrace), reflect the expanding industrial and

Greenwich Fair, 1840

commercial population of the riverside and are the first signs of the development of the Isle of Dogs since the construction of the windmills.

The 18th century witnessed the further expansion of world trade and Britain's continued involvement in wars with European rivals in which she experienced both conquest and defeat, culminating in the wars with France lasting from 1793 until 1815. The loss of the American colonies and consolidation of the British position in India were other key landmarks in the unfolding story of the Empire.

England at this time was a society of extraordinary contrasts, reflecting the continuing and deepening divide between rich and poor. Life was a mix of brutality and elegance. Bear-baiting, cock-fighting and bare-fist fighting were popular entertainments. In 1768, the year in which Sir Joshua Reynolds became founder president of the Royal Academy of Art, newspapers were also reporting the trials of Bruising Peg, "the most formidable of women pugilists." Bare-fists fights were reported on the

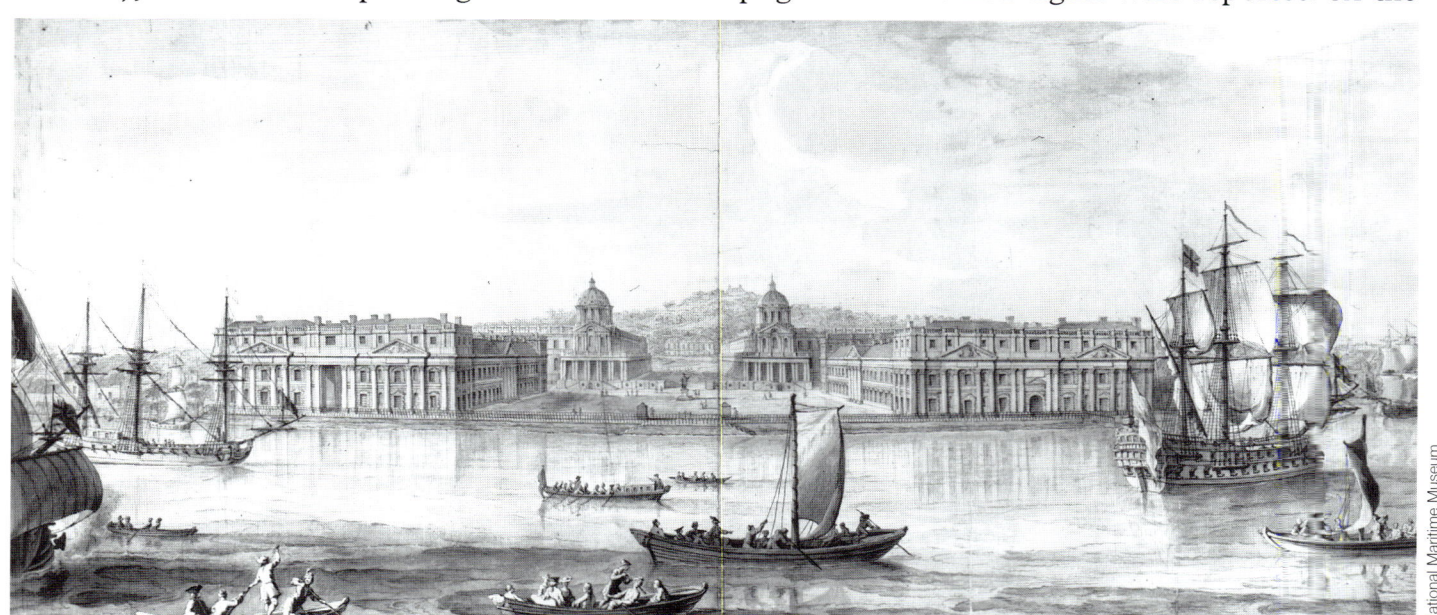

The Royal Naval Hospital at Greenwich

Dancing Bear, 1800

open fields of the Isle of Dogs in the early 19th century and almost certainly occurred there before that.

Widespread poverty, no adequate system of poor relief and no police force, combined to create a situation where petty crime was common and punishment, the only deterrent, extremely harsh. A child could be hanged for the theft of a handkerchief.

There were further improvements in general health during the century. Infant mortality fell when new lying-in hospitals and orphanages gave babies a better chance of survival. Deepening medical knowedge and the availability of cheap cotton cloth from India which could be easily washed, of pottery instead of pewter, of more and better food and cleaner streets, all made small but important differences.

Medical science had made a few advances but people still trusted old and sometimes questionable ways. Even Charles Wesley, the founder of Methodism, believed in witches and published a book on physic in which he advocated celandine under the feet as a cure for jaundice amongst other traditional remedies.

East End historian Palmer describes England at this time as "a country inclined naturally to violence" but it is important to look behind the scenes at the causes of the unrest. Changes in industry, agriculture and social life in the second half of the century have been described as "both violent and revolutionary" in their impact. They included improved transport through a network of canals and new toll roads, increased agricultural production through enclosure and new techniques, the development of the steam engine and its use in deep shaft mining, as well as the application of water power to the textile industry. These were important advances which arose from an increased understanding of science combined with the pressure of a growing population.

The rapid pace of these changes had the effect of throwing large numbers out of work - spinners, weavers, agricultural workers - whilst also creating new breeds of engineers and craftsmen, machine operatives and metal-workers. The 18th century was a time of social unrest as poverty and insecurity bit harder, especially in years of bad harvests and high prices. Growing literacy and the spread of political ideas from America and France, led to demands for greater democracy. Riots occurred all over the country around both social and political issues. In London the coal heavers rioted at Shadwell in 1760, there were disturbances amongst the Spitalfields silk weavers, and anti-Catholic riots in the 1780s. As one small example of many protests against the effects of mechanisation, a wind-driven sawmill

Blackwall Reach looking towards Greenwich, 1750

in Limehouse was wrecked by angry workers in 1768.

London was a city of particular contrasts, between the minority of elegant rich and the mass of labouring poor, with a considerable body of artisans and craftsmen forming a bridge between the two. During the century the capital acquired paved streets, lighting, a degree of sanitation and some semblance of everyday law and order, all as a result of new forms of local government. Besides being an important administrative and social centre London had many industries, including luxury trades and those producing food and clothing for mass consumption. The centre of its economy was the port, with associated services in shipping, storage, transport, finance and insurance. By 1801 its population stood at 900,000 and it had overtaken Amsterdam, its closest rival, as an international trading centre.

In the 17th century the trade of the port of London had already been greater than that of all the other English ports put together. In the 18th century growth continued at a more rapid rate than previously. The total volume of world trade was rising, and London's expanding population also added to the amount of foodstuffs and consumer goods in circulation. The capital was an internal distribution centre for flour, meal, beer, spirits, leather, glue, tallow and bacon, as well as for the exchange of raw materials and manufactured goods.

Britain has more sea coast per square mile of land than any other European country and it is hard to overstate the importance of coastal transport in an age when road transport was so slow and so costly by comparison. The majority of goods and passenger transport was by water - by canal, river or sea. Sufferance Wharves were established on the south bank of the Thames during the 18th century to supplement the hopelessly overcrowded Legal Quays, but the total length of quayside on which goods could be landed was still only 1,400 feet. Bristol, a port which handled far less trade, had almost three times as much.

The problem facing ship-owners and merchants using the port of London was straightforward, even though the solution was long in coming. There was not enough space on the Legal Quays and Sufferance Wharves for the safe and efficient mooring of vessels and the handling of cargoes. To quote from Pudney's classic history of London's docks: "In 1705 ships entering from foreign ports numbered 1,335,

tonnage 157,000; by 1751 the figures had risen to 1,682 ships, tonnage 235,000; by 1794 the numbers had shot up to 3,663 ships, tonnage 620,000... In the Upper Pool some 1,775 vessels were allowed to moor in a space laid out for about 545".

Only small craft actually discharged at the quays. Larger ships lay between Limehouse and London Bridge, at Deptford or at Blackwall. As a result, thousands of river craft were occupied in moving the cargoes from ship to shore, where goods were often left unattended and exposed to the weather. The situation was made worse by the seasonal nature of the work. The colliers arrived en masse from Newcastle, the West India fleet came all at once. The quays, warehouses and access roads surrounding the port were choked with goods in transit.

To quote Pudney again: "there was no aspect of the port that was not inefficient, exorbitant or corrupt". Merchants and ship owners suffered massive financial losses through delays, deterioration and theft. According to Patrick Colquhoun's extraordinarily detailed survey of the 1790s, the port was being systematically plundered by organised gangs which included port employees, amongst them the very revenue officers and nightwatchmen who were supposed to protect the cargoes. Colquhoun followed up his report by organising the river police at Wapping, and laying down strict rules for the employment of men working the West India cargoes.

Liverpool already had wet docks and warehouses in the Mersey and the turn-round for ships had been speeded up as a result. It was time for London to follow suit, but numerous vested interests from the City Corporation to the porters' guilds who all flourished under the existing system, delayed improvements during the 18th century. Only when the influential West India Company threatened to take its valuable trade elsewhere did the option of new docks become inevitable, and in 1799 an Act was finally passed for the construction of London's first enclosed wet docks for the loading, unloading and storage of cargoes.

Several schemes were put forward, and those chosen were William Vaughan's designs for the West India Docks and City Canal on the Isle of Dogs, and for the London Docks at Wapping.

Both schemes were major engineering and financial undertakings, carried out in the middle of the upheavals and stresses of the Napoleonic Wars (1793-1815). The London Docks were conveniently close to the City and to the Legal Quays, but had to be constructed in an area already densely built-up. The West India Docks, on the other hand, though further from the capital, were built across the sparsely inhabited, windswept pastures of Stebunheath Marsh.

The news of this proposed development would have been reported in newspapers, discussed in the drawing rooms of the city merchants and ships' captains at Limehouse and Poplar, debated in coffee houses and taverns in Poplar High Street. Some people would be well informed from the start - the West India merchants like George Hibbert, ship-yard owners such as Wigram and Green of the flourishing Blackwall yards, the major landowners like William Mellish, and Thomas Baker, the grazier of "considerable standing". Smaller landowners like "Farmer Smith" who owned three of the mills and a cattle shed in what was to become Cheval Street, might await a visit from surveyors, or communciations from a lawyer before his situation became clear.

Everyone touched by the development saw their way of life affected, adversely or otherwise. Properties for which their owners or tenants on the Isle of Dogs, Limehouse and Blackwall claimed compensation included: "timber yards, rope-grounds, ship-breakers yards, warehouses, private houses, cowsheds and a pub called *The Shipwrights' Arms*"

The porters guilds and other organisations affected by the removal of the West India trade from the Legal Quays were also among those in line to be recompensed for their loss of earnings. The City Corporation received part of its compensation for loss of revenue on the Legal Quays in their rights to revenue from the City Canal (later widened to become South West India Dock) which was designed to provide a short cut for shipping going to and from the Pool of London, by-passing the curves of Greenwich Reach and Limehouse Reach. To make sure of good communication between the new docks and the City offices and older warehouses to the west, Commercial Road was constructed in 1802, a broad street lined with elegant houses, running from Aldgate to the West India Dock Road and the dock entrance. This new highway was essential to the smooth operation of the dock system; cottages, gardens, orchards and anything else along the route, were destroyed to make way for it.

Whilst huge sums were being invested in these new enterprises by merchants and bankers and the owners of slave plantations in the West Indies, poverty and insecurity continued to mar the lives of the less fortunate people of Poplar. The records of poor law administration reveal their humble stories.

The social conditions of the 18th century created large numbers of "parish children" - evidence of the breakdown of family life caused by the social upheaval of the industrial revolution. A vivid account of the parish apprenticeship sytem and its abuses is given in

Imports from France, the Legal Quays, a cartoon of 1793

Dorothy George's book, *London Life in the Eighteenth Century* and Charles Dickens has immortalised the little chimney sweep in his novel *Oliver Twist.*

Conditions in the new textile factories of the north raised eyebrows amongst even the most hardened authorities, to the extent that an Act was passed in 1802, limiting the hours worked by children in cotton mills to 12 per day. Children as young as six were made to stand at their machines for hours at a time, and whipped if they faltered in their work. When they died their bodies, if they had no family, were cast into unmarked graves. Two parish children from Poplar were sent off to this fate. James Savage, aged seven, and William Parker, 12, were released to William Douglas and Company, Cotton Spinners of Pendelton, Cheshire, in 1790.

Most placements of Poplar parish children were local. In November 1805 John Listney who had been in the workhouse since July 1800 was released into the care of Mr John Louth at the Ropewalk, Limehouse; he also took 12-year-old John Harvey who had been in the workhouse since 1802. Sarah Mullings was ten years old when in 1808 she went into service with Mrs Williams of Pennyfields. Sarah had been in the workhouse for two years.

The wives and widows of soldiers and sailors and of prisoners at Newgate awaiting transportation, were amongst those claiming parish relief during the Napoleonic Wars. In 1791 Sarah Ladbrook explained her claim for relief for herself and her six children on the grounds that her husband Samuel, deceased, had worked as a yearly servant for Mr Stiles, a miller of Millwall. Mary Silva had been a hired servant to Mr Sutcliffe of Poplar and Blackwall at an annual wage of seven pounds thirteen shillings before she married her husband Joseph at St.Dunstan's Stepney, in 1810. They had two children. In 1815 she asked for relief saying that her husband: "has lately left her and sailed on a voyage to the West Indies". Hannah Addison, a widow, claimed relief in 1812. She had married her husband Thomas in Utoxeter about 1797 and had five children now aged 13, 9, 7, 4 and 14 months. They left Utoxeter some eight years previously and (he): "was employed as a labourer at digging the West India Docks and other suchlike work until his death in July last". Theodora Ward and her husband Richard hailed from Whitby. They were married at St. Dunstan's and had four children. He had sailed to the East Indies, and left her destitute.

Stories like these reveal the continual movement of population from the country to the capital. In 1805 Ann Lutie explained to the authorities that her husband Luke: "...was formerly a labourer in the West India Docks and left her about three years ago and that she has endeavoured to support herself but from illness was unable to do so." Luke had previously worked as a hired servant to a farmer and grazier in Nottinghamshire. Luke Linstead and his wife Mary, both deceased, left five children aged from 12 years to four months to the mercy of the parish in 1811. In 1808 they had migrated from their home in Swaffling in Suffolk to London where he "followed the business of a labourer in the East India Docks and elsewhere."

Nothing could have prepared the millers, cowherds and other inhabitants of the Isle of Dogs for the scale and complexity of the new development which now grew with impresssive speed on their very doorstep, and across the banks, ditches, lanes and meadows where they had been accustomed to work or take their leisure. An army of labourers with shovels and horses and carts, appeared, together with bricklayers and carpenters with the tools of their trades, architects, engineers and surveyors with their drawings and measuring instruments. The vast basins, impressive even today, were excavated and lined with brick, the lock entrances were constructed whilst the weight of the river was held back by coffer dams. Blocks of sturdy warehouses were erected along the north quay. High walls and a moat were built as well as a guard house and homes for the armed police who protected the ships and cargoes. There were workshops, stables and stately gateways.

The new dock and warehouse system when complete stretched from east to west across the former pastures at the northern end of the Isle of Dogs, immediately south of the higher ground of Poplar High Street. Access to the southern part of the Marsh and the Greenwich Ferry was now restricted by the lock bridges, two at each end, over which all traffic coming on and off the Marsh had to pass.

The Isle of Dogs, the old Stepney Marsh, had undergone a transformation, which had already had an impact on hundreds of lives. This was only the beginning.

Ralph Walker's Plan of the New Docks, 1802

View of Shipping at Limehouse Reach, 1793

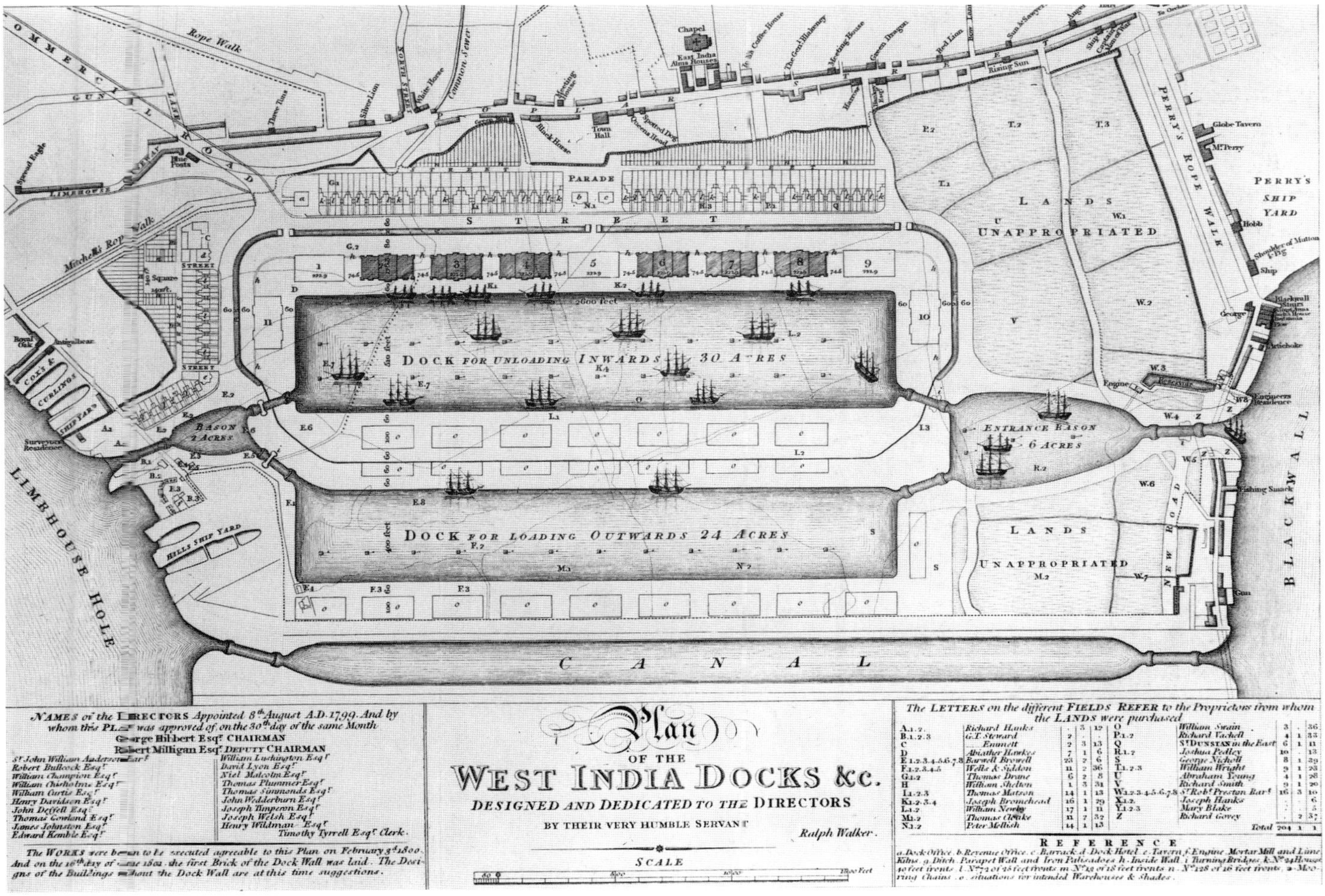

Plan OF THE WEST INDIA DOCKS &c.

DESIGNED AND DEDICATED TO THE DIRECTORS

BY THEIR VERY HUMBLE SERVANT

Ralph Walker.

SCALE

The First Industrial Phase - 1800 to the 1860s

2. Introduction

During the first 70 years of the 19th century the Isle of Dogs was transformed "from a Marsh to a Town" to quote a contemporary. Change was slow at first, the population rising from around 200 in 1800 to 1,400 in 1830. During this time, the first shipyards and small industries appeared along the Millwall embankment.

In the following 30 years, the population increased to over 14,000, streets of housing were built in both Millwall and Cubitt Town, with shops, pubs and other social amenities. A great number and variety of firms appeared all round the Island foreshore. With the construction of the Millwall Docks in the 1860s all but a few isolated remnants of open space disappeared and the change from rural settlement to urban village was complete.

The new population was made up of migrants from all over the United Kingdom and Ireland and from all walks of life. Shipbuilding, associated trades, and services for both ship-yards and the docks, were the main features of the local economy. Shipwrights and other skilled workers in related trades made up the majority of the Island's work force, a prosperous, well-organised aristocracy of labour.

This period in the Island's history came to an abrupt end in 1866, when ship-building in London was hit by a financial crisis and many yards closed, throwing thousands out of work.

These developments on the Isle of Dogs were in many respects a microcosm of changes going on in the whole of British society.

The complicated processes of the Industrial Revolution continued to work themselves out in Britain during the 19th century. The result was a society transformed from a rural to an urban population. The economy changed from agriculture and handicraft to mechanised production, with a greatly enlarged international trading base. It was an uneven transition and for some, a painful one.

Britain industrialised by exploiting natural resources of water power, coal and iron, by using existing skills and learning new ones, by continuing to engage in wars of conquest and voyages of discovery to secure new markets and new sources of raw materials.

As every schoolchild knows, coal and iron were the twin foundations of the industrial age.

Until the middle of the 18th century, iron production had depended on charcoal and only limited quantities were produced in Britain. Growing demand was met by imports but economic pressure encouraged invention and in the 1760s and 1770s new processes were discovered, making it possible to use coal, of which Britain had ample resources, in the production of large quantities of cheap but high quality iron.

The wholesale application of steam power to mining, manufacturing and agriculture, the construction of the railway network, the invention of the steamship, and the mass production of a host of domestic objects such as stoves and bedsteads, in fact, the transformation of industrial and domestic life, all stemmed from this.

The great centres of iron production developed in South Wales, the North of England and Scotland. Iron was so valuable that scrap iron became a commodity in its own right and one of the first industrial enterprises on the Isle of Dogs in the 19th century was a company processing scrap iron.

During the 19th century, through a mixture of naval power, the discipline of her soldiers, the patience of her missionaries, the guile of her diplomats and the greed of her traders, British overseas territories came to include large areas of India and Africa, as well as Egypt, added to existing colonies in Australia and Canada. Apart from these direct controlling interests, British capital was exported world-wide to finance development in Eastern Europe, Russia and South America. London, as the first city of this expanding empire, continued to grow as a port and financial and manufacturing centre.

Almost every area of everyday life in Britain was affected by the expansion of the empire. What we ate, how we dressed and what jobs and careers were opened up, were all linked to empire. Hong Kong was acquired as a result of the Opium Wars and a fashion for "Chinese drawing rooms" swept through English country mansions. Mainland China did not want to take British goods in exchange for tea and plantations in India and Ceylon were developed as an alternative source of this increasingly popular drink.

The extraordinary expansion in international trade which was to enrich Britain's position in

Making for the Thames, 1858

Victorian times depended on ships - ships to carry cargoes of raw materials and manufactured goods, and ships to protect cargoes and overseas territories. Increasingly as the century progressed, these ships were built of iron and powered by coal-fired steam engines. Steam ships carried the components of the railway, "the iron horse" across the oceans and the railways opened up the interior of vast lands, tapping sources of grain, meat and minerals previously inaccessible to Europe.

Steamships and railways also encouraged emigration and the European occupation of other lands. Between 1845 and 1855 some two-and three-quarter million people emigrated overseas from the British Isles. This exodus was prompted partly by dire conditions at home, especially in Ireland. The discovery of gold in California in 1848, and in Australia in 1851, was another major incentive.

Having always been a sea-faring nation, Britain had ship-yards all round her coast. The river Thames at the end of the 18th century was a major ship-building centre, with numerous private yards as well as the Royal Naval Dockyards at Deptford and Woolwich. The demands of the French wars (1793-1815), the continued expansion and rivalries of international trade, and the coming of steam

ships, combined to bring extra-ordinary prosperity to the Thames-side yards in the first seven decades of the 19th century, a prosperity in which the Isle of Dogs had a major share. Enterprising industrialists and inventors were to be found there, as everywhere in this age of opportunity and discovery.

Fortunes, like that of William Mellish, Island grazier and landowner, were made out of victualling ships and clothing troops for the French wars, out of mining, textiles and iron foundries; out of investment in shipping and railways at home and overseas, out of Indian tea plantations, out of the extraction of gold and silver and other precious metals. A new class of wealthy manufacturers, shipping magnates, iron founders and others emerged to challenge the monopoly of political power held by the land-owning aristocracy. This new middle class was given the vote under the Reform Act of 1832.

A swelling army of clerks, domestic servants, bailiffs, managers, lawyers, accountants, estate agents, rent collectors, insurance agents and others, made its appearance, servicing and supporting the new wealth. There were many opportunities for the investment of modest savings in small business - the retail trades, transport, storage and construction.

New modes of transport - macadamed toll roads, a network of canals and finally the railways and steamships - facilitated the movement of both goods and people. The distribution of food, cheap cotton cloth and pottery helped to improve living standards. Better health contributed to the expansion of the population from around 9 million in 1800 to 16 million in 1831 and around 20 million in 1851.

Faster communications and transport helped people to move, and most people moved away from their rural homes towards the towns and cities. The reasons for these migrations were

Gold brought from Australia by steam ship, 1850

complicated. One was simply the attractions of urban life with its opportunities for change and prosperity. Rural landlessness and impoverishment, sometimes a result of enclosures and new methods of farming, combined with the decay of handicraft production in textiles, leather, wood and metal, brought about unemployment and forced migration towards urban centres; when the rise of Yorkshire woollen mills destroyed the textile industry in East Anglia and the West Country, it was not easy for spinners, weavers, carders, carriers or even the middlemen, to find alternative work; the ending of the French wars put thousands of soldiers and sailors on the streets to beg.

In the expanding towns and cities, living and working conditions could be harsh, and got worse before they improved. Population growth and the absence of sanitation and effective urban authorities, created instant overcrowding in slum conditions. New working conditions involved long hours in gas-lit factories, driven by the iron lash of the steam engine, or back-breaking efforts to keep up with demand for coal and woollen cloth. While skilled artisans in certain trades enjoyed periods of prosperity, children and women were grossly exploited as cheap labour in the mines, in agriculture and in the textile industries.

In the first two decades of the century the distress caused by long years of war, uncertainty and social upheaval fostered political unrest and raised fears among the aristocracy and upper middle class of a repeat of the French Revolution on British soil. Repressive laws, banning trade unions and punishing political activists, were instituted but widely defied.

The 1830s and 1840s, known as the "Hungry Forties", were times of economic fluctuation. Fortunes could be lost as well as made. Insecurity, high prices, and low wages still characterised the conditions in which many people lived. Although some were concerned about poverty and hunger, it was impossible for the new Victorian entrepreneurs, any more than the old aristocracy, to foresee the years of prosperity that lay ahead. Harsh measures - the 1834 Poor Laws, imprisonment, hanging, transportation - continued to be used to control and punish hunger rioters, machine-breakers, trade unionists, strikers and the Chartists who were campaigning for universal suffrage. But Radicalism flourished in this climate of glaring injustice and deep social divisions. Though hundreds of people were

transported, trade unionism and the co-operative movement drew thousands into forms of independent working class organisation. Strong national unions of skilled workers were formed in the 1850s, with a Trades Council in every major city.

Until 1846 the Corn Laws protected farmers from foreign competition, but kept the price of bread high. The repeal of these laws, following a lively campaign, allowed cheap grain into the country and bread prices stabilised. By this time the national economy appeared to be much more secure. Britain was enjoying the fruits of successful industrialisation ahead of Europe and the United States. The country seemed set on a course of limitless expansion. There were no serious rivals in the market place - or none that could not be suppressed, which was the fate of most Indian and Irish textile producers. The Great Exhibition of 1851 confirmed Britain as "the workshop of the world" and in the boom years of the early 1850s, the value of British exports, particularly iron and steel, rose astronomically.

The boom lasted for a quarter of a century, from 1850 to 1875. There were two brief periods of financial crisis. One of these, in 1866, had a very adverse effect on life on the Isle of Dogs, and brought the first phase of its industrial development to an end.

3. Ship building on the Isle of Dogs

Shipbuilding and its associated trades were already well established in Limehouse and Blackwall at the end of the 18th century. On the Isle of Dogs the only signs of industry were Ferguson's Mast House on Millwall near the original Ile of Dogges, and Roult's Yard near Folly Wall to the east. Then the opening of the docks in 1802, the rising demand for shipping created by the French Wars (1793-1815), and the construction of West Ferry Road in 1812, combined to push forward the industrial development of the Millwall foreshore

The building and provisioning of both large and small ships became the dominant activities on Millwall until the 1860s and after a relatively slow start, by mid-century thousands of tons of vessels, of both wood and iron, powered by both sail and steam, were being launched annually from Island yards.

View of the Isle of Dogs from Greenwich in 1856, with Cubitt's yards on the north bank. Part of a larger picture.

In 1811 it was reported that: " Some very extensive iron works have been lately established at Millwall, near the Canal and West India Docks, by Jukes, Coulson and Co. In their forge and rolling mills, which are worked by two powerful steam engines, one of sixty, the other of twenty horse power, are manufactured from scrap iron, bar and bolt iron, for the use of shipbuilders and coachmakers; and iron hoops, sheet and rod iron, for home consumption and exportation; various other articles are made at the manufactory, such as anchors and mooring chains of any size; and all kinds of heavy forged iron work, for the navy and land service, for various purposes of machinery, etc."

"Near the same spot" the writer continued, "Sir Charles Price and Co. have a mill for crushing rapeseed and linseed, a turpentine distillery and a manufactory of rosin." Price's oil refinery was on the site of the two most northerly of the Millwall windmills, built in 1730 and 1740. One of them had belonged to the oil and seed broker, John Garford.

In 1817 Johnstone's *London Commercial Guide and Street Directory* listed 32 separate establishments on Millwall where previously only the mills had stood. The firms listed included Samuel Brown, the chain cable maker, Ferguson and Todd, mast makers, James Grellier, stone lime works and Greve, Grellier and Company, Roman cement manufacturers; Joad and Curling, rope-makers, C.R. and C.Price, seed crushers, and Mellish Wharf, all names which were to have a long association with the Island. The list included four mast makers, eight firms engaged in ship or barge building or as shipwrights, three ships' chandlers, three timber merchants, as well as a bread and biscuit maker, a rope maker, sail maker, cooper, brandy merchant, iron founder and chart seller. Most of these were quite small enterprises even by the standards of the day. The majority were directly connected with the building and provisioning of wooden sailing ships or barges - even the seed crushers were supplying oils for treating woodwork.

Some of the contract work undertaken by these firms may have come from within the new docks, though the dock company had their own workshops and employed dozens of craftsmen. The City Canal was used by whaling ships, laying up and restocking for their four-year voyages. They needed salt beef and Island landowner William Mellish supplied them from cattle fattened on the marsh, slaughtered and salted into casks. They needed clothing and a trader named Levy set up in business to supply them. They brought in the precious whale oil and the wax processed from spermaceti was the foundation of Price's candle works.

The ending of the wars with France led to a temporary downturn in the Island's economy. Shipbuilding for both merchant and naval fleets almost came to a standstill, and all round the country thousands of under-employed ship-wrights joined the sailors who were thrown back on the streets when they were no longer needed by the Royal Navy. Naval officers had the prospect of eking out a living on half-pay or joining one of the exploratory expeditions to Africa and the Arctic which took place in this period. Ships for these voyages were built and launched at Deptford. One of the firms supplying the Royal Navy was Brown and Lenox on Millwall, and there would have been many journeys back and forth between the two banks of the river, carrying officials, engineers and the anchors and chains which Brown and Lenox supplied. In this way Millwall's early industrial production contributed to the search for the longed-for North-West passage through the Arctic and for the source of the Niger in Africa.

The idea that iron might float had once seemed laughable but an iron boat was launched successfully on the river Severn in July 1787. Soon afterwards steam and iron were being brought together in the shipyards of the Clyde and other yards up and down the country, though it took decades of trial and error to perfect the steamship. When, after the depression of the 1820s, the shipbuilding industry as a whole revived in the 1830s, the foreshore of the Isle of Dogs proved an ideal location for new yards and new technologies. Millwall attracted many inventors and men of vision, amongst them David Napier, William Fairbairn, John Scott Russell and Isambard Kingdom Brunel.

As a young man, Scottish-born David Napier had experimented with building and fitting the first steam engines for wooden vessels, notably *The Comet*. In 1839 he established a shipyard on Millwall, approximately opposite the end of Cahir Street. With his two sons in charge of day-to-day business, Napier continued to experiment on improvements to the speed and efficiency of the iron steam boat. Like many owner-managers of the time, he and his family lived on the site in Napier House, a purpose-built villa. A fire destroyed the yard and buildings, though not the house, in 1853. David Napier and his sons returned to the Clyde in 1854 and the yard was sold to John Scott Russell, whose company built the *Great Eastern.*

William Fairbairn was once described as "one of the most eminent engineers and cultivators of mechanical science". He was born in Scotland in 1789, and was a life-long friend of George Stephenson, the famous pioneer of the railway. Fairbairn had a shipyard in Manchester,

William Fairbairn

David Napier

but in 1835 he opened another on Millwall, next door to the one bought by Napier a year or two later. It was here that Fairbairn tested and proved the idea of tubular iron bridges, leading to the rectangular cellular construction used on the Conway and Britannia bridges and many others all over Britain, about 1,000 in all, built by his firm. He left Millwall in 1848 to concentrate on his Manchester company, and his site, like Napier's yard, became part of John Scott Russell's works. He left a legacy of bridge-building and constructional engineering behind him on Millwall.

Isambard Kingdom Brunel, who went into partnership with John Scott Russell to build the giant *Great Eastern,* was another of the great inventors of his day. In the design of his vessels he tried to overcome the chief problem with the early steam-ships: how to balance their excessive coal consumption with adequate cargo-carrying capacity.

The *Great Eastern* was equipped for sail, paddle wheel and screw propulsion; it could accommodate 800 first-class passengers and over 3,000 second class. The ship was 691 feet long, 83 feet wide and 58 feet deep and was intended to steam for 45 days on 15,000 tons of coal. The construction of such a ship was one of the outstanding engineering achievements of the century. It was the longest liner until the *White Star Oceanic* in 1899 and the heaviest until the *White Star Celtic* in 1901, by which time the compound marine engine and the high-tensile steel hull had made Brunel's vision of the 1850s into the reality of the 1900s, and steam-powered ships could compete with the fastest clippers.

The story of the *Great Eastern*, the difficulties in construction, the disagreements between Scott Russell and Brunel, the problems of the launch and later misfortunes, is well known. The ship was finally launched in 1858 at the sixth attempt but it was found to be too costly to operate and too cumbersome for long voyages in rough seas. It was however, used successfully as a cable-laying ship, creating the first electric telegraph link between Europe and America and thus pioneering a new age of rapid international communication. The *Great Eastern* was last used as a travelling exhibition and fun fair and was taken to Birkenhead to be broken up in 1891.

In spite of the failure of Brunel's undertaking, the 1850s was a period of extraordinary prosperity and activity for Thames shipyards.

The intense activity of the ship-building yards on Millwall, and the new technologies employed there, attracted the attention of contemporary commentators. Their tone reflects the pride and astonishment felt by many early Victorians in the achievements of the new industrial age of iron and steam.

"The premises known as Millwall Iron Works, were fitted out in 1836, by Mr William Fairbairn, the celebrated Engineer of Manchester, and are planned upon a very extensive scale, comprising Engineers fitting and erecting shops, joiners and pattern makers' shops, iron and Brass Foundries, Smithies, a remarkably handsome chimney shaft, etc., etc.., besides every appurtenance in the yard, for constructing vessels of the largest class, both in wood and iron.

Here were built several vessels of war, for the Navy, including the *Grappler* etc. The firm are now building a frigate for H. M. government. The present proprietor is Mr Scott Russell, well known from his researches and experiments...whose name will long be remembered in connection with the Exhibition of 1851 as its indefatigable Secretary as well as one of its original promoters.

These premises possess a river frontage of great extent and are an object of great attraction to the steam boat traveller, from the interest naturally excited in witnessing so many vessels constantly in course of construction, besides which, the launches which take place here have an especial interest from the fact, that the vessels are usually fully equipped ready for sea before launching and with engines on board. This we believe to be peculiar to Millwall. Messrs Scott Russell and Company are Engineers, as well as Iron and Wood ship builders, and the only firm in London combining these usually distinct departments. They employ on an average 1,200 hands throughout the year."

This extract from Cowper's *History of Millwall (1853)* was given to him by "a gentleman connected with this large establishment" and shows that ships for the Royal Navy were being built on Millwall as well as at Deptford.

Although the sailing ship was still, in mid-century, the most efficient means of carrying cargoes to the other side of the world, steam was already in the ascendancy. The Royal Navy was keen to purchase iron-clad ships with their capacity to withstand enemy gunfire. At the same time, steam-powered ships were in great demand for short sea runs, a demand created by the Crimean War and by Britain's expanding overseas trade. The coal industry alone exemplifies the rise of steam. In 1852, 17 cargoes, amounting to 9,500 tons of coal, were brought into London by steam collier. In 1862, just 10 years later, 1,427 cargoes were carried by steam, a total of one million tons. Though the majority of steam colliers were built on the Clyde, a number were constructed in the Thames. The figures are also a reflection of the great expansion of London's population and industry, and therefore coal consumption, in this period.

The Thames yards, though more expensive than northern yards, were renowned for their reliability, and many shipping lines had their head offices in London and preferred to place their orders locally. With business prospects so good, existing firms prospered and new companies were set up.

Scott Russell built many other ships at his Millwall yard both during and after the *Great Eastern*, the last one to be launched being the *Thunderer*, a 17-knot paddle steamer reputed to be the fastest ship of the day. When Scott Russell retired, his yard was taken over by C.J.Mare, formerly of the Thames Iron Works, who established the Millwall Iron Works and Shipbuilding Company there. The letter CJM, still visible in the year 2000 on a building in West Ferry Road opposite Burrell's Wharf, date back to this time. In his book *Dockyard Economy* (1864) Barry said that he had counted 13 ships under construction at the Iron Works, and that this company and the Thames Iron Works were the only two in the country which were both

ironworks and shipbuilding works combined. The Millwall Ironworks had its own forges, steam hammers and rolling mills and was responsible for building the famous iron-plated ram, *Northumberland*. Massive cast-iron columns for bridges over the Thames were also made here.

The extent to which the entire globe was open to the enterprise and ambition of individual Victorian engineers is illustrated by the case of Welshman John Hughes. He was one of the directors of the Millwall Iron Works. In the 1860s he devised a new mounting for heavy guns which were used on the early "iron-clads"; this was so successful it became known as the "Hughes Stringer", and attracted international interest.

The Russian government ordered Millwall iron for the naval fortress they were building at Kronstadt in the Baltic. In 1864 they sent two engineers to Millwall to see the work in progress and from conversations with these men, John Hughes learned of Russia's urgent need for a domestic rail network. As a result he visited Russia and was a given a government contract to develop the coal and iron resources of the Donnetz province of Yekaterinoslav.

In 1869 John Hughes left the smoke and clangour of Millwall to found a new industrial town amongst the peasants and nomadic herdsmen of the Ukraine. Seventy skilled workers from his native South Wales, where there was high unemployment just then, went to join him there. By the 1880s the works employed 8,000 people and the company land stretched over 55,000 acres.

Another famous Millwall shipyard, and one supplying many nations, was Samuda's, in Cubitt Town. Barry wrote of it that it was: "one of the best known on the Thames and usually had in hand as much as 16,000 tons of shipping".

The Samuda brothers were descendants of Spanish/Portuguese immigrants, and started their first business in Southwark in the 1830s, building marine boilers. They moved to Blackwall in 1843. Unfortunately in 1844 Jacob Samuda and seven workers were killed in an explosion on the site. Joseph Samuda kept the company going and went on to build warships, steam packets and luxury private steam yachts. Samuda Street and the Samuda Estate recall this successful enterprise.

Yet another Cubitt Town shipyard which opened in the early 1860s was Dudgeons, of Cubitt Town - commemorated in the wharf of that name. The company started work during the

American Civil War and specialised in building blockade runners fitted with twin screws, then a new development. Between 1862 and 1865 they built 20 vessels, 12 of which were blockade runners.

Although ship-building and related trades were the dominant features of Island industry in the early and middle decades of the 19th century, other, more varied and equally rapid development was going on, reflecting the general prosperity and optimism of the national economy. In his *History of Millwall* (1853), Cowper provides a "round the Island" guide in his list of those industries which he noticed.

From Limehouse proceeding southwards were Fletcher's Dry Docks; Canal Iron Works, where "very extensive contracts have been executed for British and foreign governments"; an extensive rope manufactory; The Times brewery; Mr Salt and Mr Hill, two builders; Regent Graving Dock; Fuller's barge building yard; Steam Flour Mills; Hutchings Wire Rope Manufactory (commemorated in Hutchins Street) and the original Patent Wire Rope manufactory of Messrs Binks and Stephenson; Lamings chemical works; Blachfield's cement and terracotta works; the works and ore floors of the British and Colonial Smelting and Reduction company, "a new established firm which issued its first Plate of Silver in August, 1853"; Burney and Bellamy, makers of ships' water, bread and oil tanks; makers of corrugated iron roofs and houses "where many hundreds of dwelling have been erected, since the discovery of gold in Australia, for the accommodation of great multitudes of our fellow countrymen who have recently emigrated".

The list continued with Fenner's oil works (in later years, Fenner and Alder's paint works); Cassells' Pitch, Tar, Oil, Paint, Naptha and Varnish establishment; Brown and Lenox, manufacturer of anchor chains; Ferguson's mast and block manufacturers; Burnett's works for the manufacture of disinfecting fluid and preservation of timber, canvass, cordage etc.; the lead, colour and chemical factory of Pontifex and Wood; a pottery, newly established.

The list brings us into the newly-developing Cubitt Town where in addition to Mr Cubitt's own establishment, which included saw mills, timber wharves, cement factory and ceramic works, there were other new companies including "Johnson's rolling mills and iron works, a wharf for the manufacture of lime and storage of all kinds of construction materials, new shipyards

including the Samuda Brothers, alongside the much older Canal Docks, previously Mr Pitchers now occupied by the Soames brothers."

William Cubitt was one of the first master builders and brother of the better-known Thomas who developed parts of Belgravia and Pimlico in west London. The Cubitts had moved to London from their Norfolk home early in the 19th century. William's chief interest lay in the construction of large public buildings, such as Covent Garden Market and King's Cross Station. However, during these decades of Victorian prosperity, he also master-minded the development of Cubitt Town with its industries and streets of terraced houses.

One of the oldest and most enduring of Island firms mentioned in Cowper's list, and one closely connected to ship-building, was Brown Lenox and Company, manufacturer of iron cable chains. Samuel Brown had been a fellow officer of Nelson during the French Wars. Whilst in the Navy, he had realised that a chain of iron links would be a better way of mooring ships than the hemp ropes which were then in use. He patented the stud link chain in 1808 and it was adopted for naval use in 1810.

Brown Lenox were the sole manufacturers of chains for the Navy until 1916 - the longest ever unbroken Admiralty contract. The company moved to Millwall in 1812 from Narrow Street, in Ratcliffe. The new site was chosen because of its location on the riverbank opposite the naval dockyard at Deptford, the firm's largest customer. By 1818, the business was growing so rapidly that Brown Lennox had to expand into a six-acre site at Pontypridd, next to the Glamorgan Canal, and close to sources of coal and iron. This site continued in operation after the Millwall branch closed down in 1981.

During the 19th century the firm earned a reputation as a premier manufacturer of ships' cables and berth moorings for the most turbulent harbours and rivers of the world. They supplied cables to many foreign governments and for the largest ships of their time, including the *Great Eastern*, the *Mauretania* and the *Acquitania*. Altogether, thousands of tons of cables, anchors and mooring buoys were made at the Millwall works. The first cable-testing machine, capable of testing chains up to 100 tons tension, was erected here, and was still in daily working order over 100 years later. Brown Lennox is also noted for having constructed the first suspension bridge in the country, across the Tweed at Berwick.

Another firm mentioned above was Binks and Stephenson, wire-rope manufacturer. George Binks is credited with having invented a method of twisting fine strands of wire into rope whilst he was foreman ropemaker at Woolwich Dockyard in the 1830s. His first factory was in Great Grimsby, Lincolnshire, but as the value of his invention was gradually recognised, he was able to establish a much larger works on Millwall, where he was joined by his son, Jabez Binks.

There were hundreds of minor inventors in this age of Victorian expansion, most of them long-since forgotten. One of these was William Roberts, the son of a Deptford shipwright. In the 1860s William lived in a house at the Brown & Lenox works where he was employed as a foreman anchorsmith. He was also an inventor,

London Fire Brigade

William Roberts' Fire Engine, Millwall, 1860s

specialising in the design and manufacture of pumps, fire engines and hoses. By 1867 he had his own works, and was described as : "patentee and manufacturer of steam and hand fire engines, hose reels, pumps, testing and hydraulic machinery, boilers and steam cranes, traction and portable engines, valves, hydrants, standpipes, etc., parallel vices with adjusting jaws, iron and brass founders, coppersmith, etc. at West Ferry Road, near the pier, Millwall". In the 1871 census, his address is given as 25 Kingsbridge Place and he was recorded as "Engineer Founder, employing 22 men and two boys".

William Roberts is credited with the design and construction of the first European self-propelled steam fire engines. His machines were exhibited at show trials in the 1860s and in 1865 he built a special engine to order for the Arsenal in Rio de Janeiro. This engine, the *Excelsior,* was

put through its trials at Millwall before being shipped to South America.

William Roberts, Samuel Brown, John Hughes, Napier, Fairbairn, Scott Russell – theirs are some of the success stories of the Industrial Revolution on the Isle of Dogs. There were many others, but probably an equal number of failures in that time of invention, adventure and risk. James Ash was employed as a naval architect by C.J.Mare at the Millwall Iron Works for 11 years and for the Thames Iron Works for a further six years. In 1862 he started his own yard on the foreshore in Cubitt Town with offices on the corner of Pier Street, an establishment as impressive as any existing Thames shipyard. One of his customers was the Peninsular and Orient Line, but this did not protect him from bankruptcy when the industry collapsed.

By the middle of the 19th century iron, coal and steel were being increasingly used in ship-building, as we have seen. The Thames shipyards lay far from the main sources of these essential materials and the cost of coal in London was twice as high as in the north-east, in spite of rapid and regular transport by steam collier. During the days of prosperity, a trend for orders to flow more and more to the shipyards of the north had gone largely unnoticed by investors. By 1866 the combination of high overheads and falling orders had its inevitable outcome in bankruptcies and closures, among the victims being both small concerns like James Ash and the much larger Millwall Iron Works. The effects of this disaster were felt by many lesser firms and tradesmen who had been dependent on contract work from the bigger companies and reverberated right through the Island economy to the humblest shop-keeper and the poorest labourer and his family.

Dudgeons and Samuda's struggled on for a few more years, but the prosperous days of the Thames ship-building industry were effectively over. Only yards building small, specialised craft, or repairing ships, were to survive in the long term.

One promising enterprise which was caught in the sudden economic downturn was the Millwall Dock and Canal Company. Established in 1864 just at the peak of prosperity, and when most of the Island's river frontage was already occupied, it was set up with intention of creating additional wharf space for new industries, where ships and barges could load and unload without the inconvenience of high and low tides. A T-shaped dock was planned, with entrances from the Thames to east and west. However, the company's finances were badly damaged in the crash of 1866 and there was little take up of the wharf space. In the event, only an L-shaped dock was built, with a lock entrance in West Ferry Road near Kingsbridge. Instead of becoming a hive of industrial production, the new dock joined the existing system of the London docks, providing a cargo-handling service. It was used chiefly for imports of grain and timber.

The building of the Millwall Dock had both immediate and long term effects on the Island. 3,000 navvies were employed in its construction, housed in temporary barracks on the site. Most of the earth which they excavated was not carted away, but was deposited round the edge of the dock basins, raising them above the level of the surrounding land by over ten feet. The new dock effectively divided the Island in half down the middle, although a right of way across the Inner Basin, linking the two halves of Glengall Road, was retained in the form of a rolling bridge. It took up most of the remaining pasture-land in the centre of the Island and cordoned off a large area of land which was never used for the planned eastern arm of the dock. Instead it became a dumping ground for silt, then a patchwork of allotments and eventually, the Mudchute Community Park and Farm

The new dock brought dock work - and associated activities such as transport and storage - into the heart of the Island, and it became home to McDougall's Flour, one of the Island's most famous food processing companies, and to Hooper's cable-making works, creating new jobs to replace some of those which disappeared with the collapse of ship-building. It also prompted the construction of the Island's own passenger railway service, the Millwall Extension Railway.

In 1866 the Island's first industrial phase, the age of iron masters, inventors and great ships, was effectively over. But it was still an industrial village, close to the capital and at the heart of a busy international port where small boat and barge building, as well as ship repair work, could prosper. At the same time growth was to continue in the engineering, manufacturing, storage and processing companies which had grown up alongside the early shipyards and the docks.

The Lock Gates at Millwall Dock, 1868

4. Roads, Railways, Homes

An effective transport system was important to the success of the industrial growth of the Isle of Dogs. When the Island foreshore was developed, part of its attraction was that the new industrialists were able to make use of existing waterways. The Thames was a highway in itself, and from Limehouse the Regent's Canal gave access to the national canal network, developed in the 18th century and providing faster and more reliable inland communications than the roads, many of which were in poor repair.

In the 19th century riverside wharves were extended or created all round the Island from Limehouse to Blackwall to accommodate the increasing traffic in barges and lighters. In 1850, for instance, work was carried out by Pontifex and Wood (later Associated Lead) to form an embankment 550 feet in length at their riverside factory in Westferry Road. In the 1860s the firm was again given permission by the Thames Conservancy Board to carry out improvements to "make the shore safe for barges". This was typical of many similar operations and in this way the Island was gradually ringed with wharves.

As goods traffic increased so did passenger ferry services up and down and across the river. Cowper (1853) records the ferry plying places along Millwall. These were at Regent Wharf, Torrington Arms, King's Arms, Tindall's Dock and Ferry Street. The latter was the old-established Potter's Ferry and all the others had come into being as industry spread along the embankment.

Cowper noted that: "There was a Ferry called Willow Bridge Ferry, near Messrs Ferguson's Works, but this is obsolete." This may have been Deptford Ferry, used by Pepys and if so it is hard to believe it had fallen out of use. In the hey-day of Island ship-building, communications were frequent between the engineering works, anchor-smiths, mastmakers, etc., of Millwall, and the Royal Naval yards at Deptford. In later years Deptford Ferry suffered varied fortunes, including a failed attempt to start up a steamboat service. There was still a limited passenger service to Deptford at the beginning of the 20th century, recalled by stevedore George Pye as costing one penny. All traces of this ancient river crossing have now disappeared apart from the cul-de-sac of Deptford Ferry Road almost opposite Cahir Street.

Industrial development brought an increase in road traffic - pedestrians getting to and from work, street sellers, horse-drawn wagons laden with goods, the private carriages of merchants and factory owners, hand carts and messengers on horseback. The Island's old roads were unsuited to industrial traffic. There was a track from Limehouse along the top of the river wall past the windmills as far as the ferry to Greenwich. This old road cut right through the potential development area of the foreshore and river bank. Another ancient road to the ferry to Greenwich led down Harrow Lane in Poplar High Street and across Stebunheath Marsh past the settlement near the site of the medieval chapel, but it did not give access to the Millwall area.

To improve access to the Millwall foreshore and to the Greenwich ferry, West Ferry Road was built as a toll road in 1812 on the initiative of local businessmen. An Act of Parliament was passed, giving subscribers to the venture the right to: "establish a common ferry of one or more boats, for horses, carriage, cattle, goods, ware and merchandise, from Wood Wharf Greenwich to Ferry House, Isle of Dogs." Under the terms of the Act the investors were also obliged to : "pave, maintain, widen and keep in repair a new convenient carriage road leading from the north side of the premises of Sir Charles Price, baronet, near the bridge at the west end of the canal of the Isle of dogs and from hence in and through Poplar Marsh, otherwise Stebunheath Marsh, to the river Thames..."

Among those who put up the money for the new road were Sir Charles Price, George Byng, the Reverend William Tooke, William Mellish, Robert Batson and Augustus Ferguson, all local businessmen and landowners whose names have survived on wharves or streets. The northern section of the new road was first named Mill Wall Road, then Bridge Road and Ord Street, and the southern section, from where the old *Three Arms* stood, "Deptford and Greenwich Ferry Road". Eventually it became Westferry Road along its entire length from West India Dock Road to Millwall Fire Station.

The Island's other main perimeter road, Manchester Road, came into being on the initiative of one man, William Cubitt, as part of the development of Cubitt Town in the 1840s and 1850s.

The agreement between Cubitt and the main landowner, the Countess of Glengall (who had inherited the estate of her father, William Mellish) stipulated that as part of the general improvement of the area he should build a carriageway sixty feet wide (which the Countess was to be able to use free of charge), and this was duly done. The difference in the width of the two roads is still very apparent.

In 1858 the Island bathed in the glare of publicity sparked off by attempts to launch the *Great Eastern*. An article in *The Builder* in February of that year described "the primitive-looking toll house composed of waste timber thickly pitched" and remarked that "Omnibuses and cabs are already plying from the city to the Isle of dogs." Dickens, writing in 1853, referred to crossing from Greenwich by the ferry and taking "the smallest of all metropolitan omnibuses from Millwall to Limehouse", the Island's first bus service.

The road to the ferry from Poplar through Harrow Lane eventually became the modern East Ferry Road. It was realigned eastwards when the West India Docks were built in 1800, and effectively became part of Preston's Road as far as the lock bridges. It then ran south to pick up its original course past the site of the old chapel to the river bank. When the Millwall Docks were excavated in the early 1860s the remains of the chapel and surrounding buildings were demolished to make way for a graving dock and the old road was again realigned eastwards. (It remained in place until it was moved again in 1998 to make room for a new Docklands Light Railway station at Mudchute. East Ferry Road, also known locally as Farm Road, still ends, as it has for hundreds of years, at *The Ferry House* pub on the river bank).

The new West Ferry Road was an improvement in its day but its narrow width contributed to the congestion problems of the 20th century. From the beginning an even greater problem for road transport on and off the Island lay with the lock bridges, wide enough for only a single lane of traffic.

Limehouse Basin at the western end of the West India Docks provided access for barges and lighters between the river and the new docks. A single lock and road bridge led from the river into the Basin, from which two more locks led into the import and export basins. A few hundred yards further south, another lock gate and bridge linked the Thames and the new City Canal, built across the Island to provide a short cut for sailing ships between Blackwall and Limehouse. That lock entrance still survives near the *City Pride* (formerly the *City Arms*) public house. At the eastern end of the dock basins and canal, two further lock gates and bridges gave access to and from the Thames for shipping. (The more southerly of these entrances is still in use as the modern "Blue Bridge").

Traffic was frequently held up at these four lock entrances. When the Millwall Docks were built in the 1860s, a fifth lock entrance in West Ferry Road caused still more delays. "Catching a bridger" became a common experience and contributed to the Island's relative isolation from the rest of East London. The chaos and confusion of horses, carts and carriages, riders, pedestrians, hand-barrows, combined with the occasional herd of cows or sheep from the pastures and even from time to time caged circus animals being brought from the docks, all waiting in a disorderly queue for ships and barges to be manoeuvred through the locks, is not hard to imagine. The air must have been blue sometimes. Nothing was done to alter this bottleneck situation until the end of the 19th century.

The West India Docks were linked to the City of London and the offices and warehouses near the Pool by the river Thames and by the new Commercial Road which led via the East India and West India Dock Roads straight into the docks at either end. Commercial Road was fitted with stone tramways to speed up the passage of horse-drawn vehicles.

The new roads were used by the many shippings agents, insurance brokers and merchants who had their offices and warehouses in the city and who needed to keep in constant touch with their vessels and cargoes in the West and East India Docks. Clerks and messengers boys, ships' captains and crews, ship owners, passengers for sailing ships to the West and East Indies, customs officers and salesmen, all travelled in increasing numbers between London and Blackwall in carriages and hackney cabs.

By 1837, two million passengers used this form of transport annually, the journey taking 40 minutes by carriage, an hour by omnibus. Goods destined for storage in city warehouses were carried either seven miles by the river (an estimated 160,000 tones in 1837) or by horse-drawn transport four miles along Commercial Road (an estimated 180,000 tons in 1837).

Statistics like these helped to attract investment into a railway - then an entirely new form of transport - between the Minories near the Tower of London and the new passenger steamer terminal at Brunswick Wharf, Blackwall. The consulting engineer was William Cubitt, whose other projects in the capital included

Emigrants preparing to board a vessel at Brunswick Pier, 1849

Covent Garden Market and King's Cross Station and who was about to become heavily involved in the development of the eastern side of the Island.

The new railway, which was opened in 1840, had a number of distinctive features. It was built on a brick viaduct, allowing it to pass through crowded districts with minimum disruption; it used cable haulage for the first few years of its operation; and it is also noted for being one of the first commercial users of the new electric telegraph. After a few years of independent existence the Blackwall Railway became absorbed into the developing system of railways linking the docks with the national network. (Parts of the original brick viaduct were incorporated into the construction of the Docklands Light Railway in the 1980s).

The opening of the Millwall Dock in 1868 prompted the introduction of a steamer service between the city and Millwall Pier, and an omnibus service, which ran every 15 minutes between West India Dock Station and Millwall Dock entrance to meet trains on Blackwall Railway to Fenchurch Street.

William Hart was a cooper, born in 1776. He learned his trade in Luton, and after working in St. Albans for a time decided to move to London, where he had an uncle at Shadwell: "having been to see my uncle several times and seen so much work and great wages earned in the Cooper's trade, it being still war time." He had to work very hard to earn the "great wages", but eventually found employment with the West India Dock company, where he remained for 30 years.

His autobiography includes an account of how, whilst working in Shadwell, he came to rent a house. It also casts light on other circumstances of the time.

"(I)went to lodge in Shadwell Market with one Mr Frith, who had been a shopmate. This was July 26th, 1800. Here I was very comfortable, having a room and a bed for myself and very near work. This is no small matter when a man works by the piece, as much time is saved by walking backward and forward, but a greater benefit than this was being so near my work I was sheltered from the danger of being pressed for a sailor, as the French war was at the hottest all this time... I continued to lodge with Mr Frith for about seven months when he, having little property, went into business in Whitecross Street. Here I was put to my shifts. To go to lodge with strange people after being so comfortable was very disagreeable to me. While I was at work one day thoughts suggested to my mind that I should like to take the house myself, it being a small one, having three rooms and a kitchen and a bit of garden and being in a decent neighbourhood, also very cheaply rented and taxed. The rent was £6.00 per annum and taxes and water about £1.4.0. more. This was very cheap at the time, as rents were rising owing to the pulling down of many houses for the London Docks."

Later, after his marriage, William Hart bought a house for his family in St.George's East where they lived until he was pensioned off at the age of 56.

The construction and opening of the West India Docks, the City Canal, the associated road works, and the industrial development of the Millwall foreshore, created new employment opportunities for the area, attracting newcomers and creating a demand for more living space. The importance which William Hart attached to living close by his work would have been common to most. Many of those employed to handle cargoes in the new docks lived to the north of the Marsh, since there was very little housing on the Marsh itself, and the main point of access into the dock area was from the north in West India Dock Road. These newcomers would have added to already crowded conditions in the poorer quarters of the old settlements of Poplar, Limehouse, Stepney and Bow or even further afield - anywhere within walking distance. Clerical and skilled workers employed in the docks, like William Hart, also found lodgings, normally of a better quality, in these riverside villages.

Up to the 1830s, housing development proceeded slowly on the Isle of Dogs. In 1831 the population had risen from about 200 in 1800 to 1,344 and the number of inhabited houses was only 230. In the 1830s the land on the eastern side of the Marsh was still all fields and reed beds.

There were older cottages near each of the windmills, at the Ferry House, the Mast House and at Roult's yard near Folly Wall. A large acreage of pasture remained in the interior and sometime after 1817 a John Hodgson leased land from William Mellish near the old chapel where he built himself a house and eight cottages which he sub-let. These buildings were later demolished to make way for Millwall Dock. The earliest industrial housing on Millwall consisted of short rows of cottages which were built alongside the new West Ferry Road and beside workshops and shipyards on the riverside.

A number of villas were built by Island businessmen in order that they too could live near their workshop or shipyard, since transport by private carriage or horseback was slow and tedious. This was typical of the early stages of the industrial revolution, an echo of pre-industrial times when employer and workers of necessity lived close together or under the same roof.

Lawn House, near the entrance to the City Canal, was built in 1818 for his own use by Thomas Pitcher, a shipbuilder who had leased the Canal Dry Docks on the riverside of Manchester Road. When the lease of the house was sold in 1848 it was described as: "A spacious and very commodious modern residence with lawns and gardens stocked with fruit trees, coach house, stables, offices and yard." Pitcher also had a row of cottages, Canal Row, built nearby for his chief workmen. Another large family home was Napier House in Napier Yard, built by David

London Metropolitan Archive

Napier House, West Ferry Road 1975

Napier in the 1830s. It was square, with a columned porch and had its own orchard and garden.

Between 1840 and 1860 the pace of house-building quickened, bolstered by the demand created by thousands of new jobs in shipbuilding and engineering along the Millwall foreshore and the simultaneous development of Cubitt Town on the eastern side of the Island. In the 1840s the area was, in the words of William Baker, clerk to the Commissioners of Sewers for Stebunheath Marsh, going through "a transition from a Marsh to a Town". By the 1860s the population had risen to over 14,000. The number of inhabited buildings was 1,688 and almost the entire stock of Victorian housing was in place. This rapid growth in housing and population matched the economic expansion of the Island and the country as a whole.

The first streets of terraced houses to be built

on the Island were Alfred Street and Robert Street, off West Ferry Road immediately to the south of the City Canal and later renamed Manilla Street and Cuba Street in recognition of the Island's profitable connections with those West Indian Islands.

The houses in Alfred Street were four-roomed, "two up, two down", with an added scullery and, out in the back yard, a closet (lavatory). At this time, closets were normally "dry". Contents were neutralised with earth or ashes and collected regularly by "night-soil men" to be carted away into the countryside. If there was a cold water supply (not likely until after mid-century) it was in the scullery which also housed the copper and perhaps a cooking range, though this may have been in the back room. There was probably a small fireplace - rarely used - in each of the other rooms.

Housing on the Island never kept up with demand, and from the census of 1851 we can see that these houses were already filled to bursting with the families of new Islanders. There were 63 houses in the street, with a total population of 461, out of whom 151 were children under 12 years of age. 37 of the houses were occupied by one family, in some cases quite a large family. 18 houses had two families each, seven were occupied by three families each and one house contained four separate households. There were 18 lodgers, all unmarried men.

There was nothing unusual at the time about this multiple occupancy, most people were used to living in cramped conditions with little privacy. William Roberts, who worked at Brown & Lenox and had his own business building fire engines, lived at No.11 Tooke Street, Millwall, in 1851. His household in what was probably a three-bedroomed house included his wife and their three daughters, his stepson from his wife's first marriage, his widowed sister and her daughter.

Land on Millwall was in the hands of several individuals and was leased in small parcels to speculative builders for housing, pubs and shops which they then sold on to private landlords for sub-letting. John Henry Weitzel and his business partner Nicholas Knight were typical examples. They were publicans at *The Ironmongers' Arms* in Westferry Road in 1857. They leased a piece of land nearby from the Ironmongers' Company and built Ingleheim Terrace, "15 good and substantial houses" on it. They engaged James Hutchins, a bricklayer, of Manchester Road, to build two of the houses and one shop.

In this way, through many individual investments, the side streets of Millwall and the length of Westferry Road, were built up during the 1850s and 1860s. Styles varied between flat-fronted and bay-windowed, two- and three-bedroomed, but there were no basements here as there were in Cubitt Town. The names of the terraces in Westferry Road reflect local and national loyalties - Ebenezer Terrace, Strafford Place, Albert Place, Victoria Place, Arthur Terrace, William Terrace (which is still there), Adelaide Place, Prince Patrick Place, Kingsbridge Place and Manchester Terrace. In 1875 the road became Westferry Road along its entire length and the original names of the terraces became redundant.

On the eastern side of the Island the development was much more the inspiration of one man, William Cubitt. His involvement with the Blackwall railway brought him to East London and the open spaces of the eastern side of the Isle of Dogs with its mile of undeveloped and valuable foreshore. With a sharp eye for a profitable investment, he leased 120 acres of land here, most of it from the Countess of Glengall. He installed his own builders' yard; he sub-let the remaining river frontage for industrial use; he devised a layout of new streets and built Manchester Road; he played a substantial role in building Christ Church; and sub-let the rest of

William Cubitt, Lord Mayor of London

the land for house building. Part of his holding was the "Twenty-Acre Field" on which Sysell Street, Kingfield Street, Billson Street and Parsonage Street were eventually built.

The development of Cubitt Town followed the same pattern as Millwall, with industry by the river and housing on the inland side of the perimeter road. Cubitt Town was rather more spaciously laid out and some of the houses, with basement floors below the level of the street and stairs up to the front door, had a simple elegance and uniformity - which unfortunately concealed damp cellars liable to flooding and the use of cheap materials generally.

Although the overall plan was Cubitt's, there were many smaller investors in Cubitt Town, just as there were in Millwall. Investment in working-class housing offered only a low return, but required a relatively small amount of initial capital. Thomas Cubitt said that a tenemented house was a good investment for: "a little, shop-keeping class of persons who have saved a little money in business...I think very few persons of great capital have anything to do with (poor people's houses) at all." However we have seen that, although not directly involved in the business of building the houses and collecting rents from the poor people, "persons of great capital" were involved, as freehold landowners, in leasing out land to developers - the Earl of Strafford on Millwall and the Countess of Glengall in Cubitt Town being two examples.

Charles Davis, who leased land in Manchester Road, was typical of Thomas Cubitt's "little, shop-keeping class of person". He paid no rent in the first year, during which time he had houses built, buying materials on credit from Cubitt's yard. Once the houses were occupied, which they were almost before the mortar had dried, he began to recoup his outlay and pay his rent and outstanding debt to Cubitt or Cubitt's Estate.

Davis lived in Manchester Road on the corner of Samuda Street, was the landlord of *The Manchester Arms* and had Davis Street named after him. In 1861 he was recorded as the owner of three terraces in Manchester Road as well as houses in Samuda Street and Stewart Street. Another landlord who lived locally was Henry Hewlett, of Stewart Street, who owned numbers 15 to 23 inclusive. Others were from further afield, like Mr Bliss, of Lambeth who owned houses in Stewart Street and Davis Street, Mr Jordan of Poplar and Mr Gable of Commercial Road, both of whom owned houses in Manchester Road.

The bay-windowed and three-storeyed houses were intended for the families of skilled artisans and white collar workers, while the smaller terraced houses in the side streets were built for unskilled labourers. William Cubitt also had a few villas built which were suitable for the local middle class, along Saunders Ness Road overlooking the river and Greenwich.

The terraced cottages, the commodious villas, the wide streets, the orchard, gardens and remaining pastures, the river, the pleasing impression conveyed by these words does not make up the complete story of Island housing in the first half of the 19th century. Thomas Wright described the Island in the 1860s as having: "slushy, ill-formed roads, tumble-down buildings, stagnant ditches and tracts of marshy, rubbish-filled waste ground" giving quite a different picture, and he added that it was also unpleasantly smelly because of its "chemical works, tar manufactories and similar establishments."

Much of the Island was a building site for most of the middle decades of the century, a building site on a damp, low-lying marsh, liable to flood and criss-crossed by open drains which were rapidly turning into domestic and industrial sewers. Most of the roads were unmade and there were no pavements - women walked about in pattens to keep their long skirts out of the mud.

The great yards were a dangerous jumble of machinery, timber and sheds, with the ever-present danger of fire. Scott Russell's yard had a smithy, steam shaping and cutting machinery worth £12,000 a three- storey building 150 feet by 100 feet, a carpenters shop, 90 x 25 feet; engine and boiler fitting sheds, tool warehouses and 1,000 tons of timber. Much of this was destroyed in fires which swept the yard on three successive occasions in the 1850s.

By the 1860s the new public authorities - the District Board of Works, the Medical Officer of Health - were hard at work trying to bring about improvements in street cleaning, rubbish clearance, drains and the supply of piped water. It was an uphill task, though less so on the Island than in the crowded quarters of the older inner city.

When the urban population of the United Kingdom began to rise dramatically in the late 18th and early 19th centuries, there was still only a glimmering of understanding about the connection between good drains, clean water, clean air and good health. The medieval systems of open drains, dunghills, cess pits and night soil collectors still operated almost everywhere. Never particularly efficient, these traditional arrangements broke down under the strain of industrialisation. There were no effective regulations to control overcrowding in existing dwellings or to impose standards on new building. Cesspits and drains quickly became blocked and stank horribly; water sources were polluted. The consequences were outbreaks of infectious diseases, nothing new in themselves, but disastrous in the crowded slums of the cities. For centuries the squalor in which the poor lived had been accepted (by the rich if not by the poor themselves) as an inevitable fact of life about which little could be done, other than charity for the meek and harsh treatment for the unruly. The social upheavals of the industrial revolution forced a change of attitude. Cholera and typhoid epidemics of massive proportions spread to threaten even the health of the better off. The Government set up Committees of Enquiry to explore the situation and devise a remedy.

Responsibility for the provision and maintenance of such public services as there were lay at this time with a variety of local bodies, most of which were neither democratic nor accountable. In Stebunheath Marsh the Commissioners for Sewers, set up in medieval times, were officially responsible for the upkeep of the embankment and the land drains.

The Commissioners had the right to impose a rate and employed a bailiff to assess repairs and recruit labour. They also employed a Clerk for their accounts, minutes and correspondence. In 1834 this was William Baker junior (his father had been Clerk before him) and he was called to give evidence before a Government Select Committee. From his evidence it was apparent that though the Commissioners met regularly for dinner their powers were too limited to cope with the drainage problems created by the docks, industry and housing which were spreading across the old pastures. William Baker was optimistic though: he assured the Select Committee that the open sewers could be cleaned by letting the water in on one side of the level and letting it out again on the other; that the atmosphere in the district was generally healthy and that he had never heard it said that the water in the docks was offensive.

In the reports of these Select Committees, the inadequacy of existing services was revealed and in the 1850s new authorities were created

and many of the old ones were swept away. But it was to be decades before the effects of overcrowding, poor quality buildings and lack of basic amenities were to be overcome. It was hard for the new authorities to erode traditional practices, and builders and landlords were reluctant to spend money on improvements which tenants might be unable to pay for in higher rents. Even on the relatively newly-built Isle of Dogs, which already had some kind of drainage system, the Medical Officer of Health for South Poplar found plenty to complain about. In May 1861 he wrote to the local Board of Works about Thomas Street, West Ferry Road, saying:

"There are 28 houses without drainage; 9 on the south side which drain into cesspools, and 14 on the north side which drain into an open ditch at the back of the houses; it is a most intolerable nuisance and in hot weather will be injurious to

London Metropolitian Archive

Early 19th century cottages, West Ferry Road, 1930s

the health of the inhabitants in that neighbourhood." Later in the same month the MOH submitted a long list of houses in Cubitt Town which had been reported as: "not having any water laid on to the closets...many of which are very foul and offensive."

These are just two examples out of many which illustrate the efforts of the MOH to raise standards.

Only in the 1860s did piped water become available to Islanders as an alternative to a bucket dipped in the Thames. This luxury was supplied at standpipes, turned on for 15 minutes daily by the East London Water Company, who, however, were not renowned for the purity of their product.

Against what seem like horror stories from a 21st century point of view, we have to set the fact that migrants arriving on the Isle of Dogs in the first half of the 19th century were not necessarily accustomed to anything better than the conditions they found there. For some, their new homes were an improvement on the rural hovels or overcrowded and tumbledown tenements they had left behind them. They drank beer or tea made with boiled water rather than fresh water. And though the industrial revolution brought pollution and overcrowding, it also brought the benefits of cheap cotton cloth and pottery, soap, oil cloth and kitchen utensils for those who could afford them, as well as the better distribution of basic foodstuffs.

For skilled workers who earned regular wages in the Island shipyards and factories in the middle decades of the century, the discomforts and smells of life on Stebunheath Marsh could be shut out of a comfortable cottage home, stuffed with furniture and well supplied with ale and tea, bread and ham, with curtains at the windows and coal in the coal-hole under the stairs.

5. All Kinds of People

"If from the top of Observatory Hill we have a penny peep through a pensioner's telescope and direct it to a greenish looking spot on the Middlesex shore, we may learn that this is the Isle of Dogs; but neither dogs nor men are to be seen there and we wonder how on earth such an uninhabited island came to be pitched down between busy Blackwall and busy Limehouse. On further examination we find it to be a low, level marshy field, fringed with factories and taverns and inhabited by a few cows. There may possibly be half a dozen trees..." Charles Dickens, *Household Words* (May 1853).

From the heights of Greenwich the Island may have appeared uninhabited and desolate but there were 5,000 people living there by 1851, most of them newcomers from towns, villages and seaports up and down the country. They found themselves living a few miles from London, between the river Thames and the marshy pastures, in newly-built homes, participating in grand undertakings at the forefront of the new industrial age. The gleaming brick and stonework of the dock walls, the warehouses and workshops, the movement of shipping, the rumble of machinery and the throb of the mighty steam engines, the thrill of seeing ships launched from Millwall or Deptford on expeditions into unknown waters, the strange people, animals and cargoes which passed through, the construction of houses, shops, pubs, wharves and factories which went on at an accelerating pace in the middle decades of the century, combined to make the Island a lively place to live, even if it was rather damp and muddy.

The development of Cubitt Town, the opening of the Millwall Dock and the prosperity of the shipyards attracted even greater numbers of migrants in the 1850s and early 1860s and as we have seen already, the population grew to over 14,000 in the 1860s. Who were these people and where did they come from?

One of the earliest surviving records of new Islanders is the baptismal register for the Island's Congregational Chapel, which was opened in 1817. With 15 entries between 1823 and 1836, and no occupations or addresses listed, it provides only fragmentary information. The names include Crummie, Prior, Lessey, Moir, McCullock, Watson, Alcock, Penn, Gewer and Rither and are those of the earliest industrial Islanders. As the first streets had not even been built then, and Cubitt Town was still a field, these families with their new-born infants were living in cottages along West Ferry Road and on the river bank. They may have been newcomers or may equally have been living on the Island before the docks were built. They may have come with drovers from the north. George Hames, born into an established Island family in the 1890s, said that his people were: "said to have been cattle and horse breeders from Bourne Fen in Lincolnshire."

The population of London as whole was growing rapidly throughout these years, reaching nearly two-and-a-half million by 1851. This growth came about partly by natural increase but also by large numbers of migrants streaming steadily into the capital from all parts of the country. Some were escaping from rural poverty and unemployment. Some followed an employer like Napier or Fairbairn to the Isle of Dogs, others moved to join friends or relations who had already migrated. London offered many opportunities for both skilled and labouring work in the expanding industries, construction projects and services.

Patchy information about individual migration in the early 19th century is available through poor law records, as we have seen, and through the rare autobiography like that of William Hart, who was attracted by the "great wages" available for skilled workmen in the capital. People were still flooding into London in mid-century and journalist Henry Mayhew recorded some of their stories. One was a young woman:

"Her father was a dock labourer and had been every since he came to London, which he did some years ago, when there was great distress in Rochdale, where he worked in a cotton factory; but being starved out there after working short time for some weeks, he tramped with his daughter, then about fourteen, up to town, and could get nothing to do but work in the docks, which requires no skill, only a good constitution and the strength and endurance of a horse. This however, as every one knows, is a precarious sort of employment, very much sought after by strong, able-bodied men out of work. The docks are a refuge for all Spitalfields and the adjacent parishes for men out of work, or men whose trade is slack for a time". The man had suffered a broken arm and injured spine through a keg of spirits falling on him and was in hospital. His daughter had become a prostitute in order to support him.

Mayhew also recorded the case of a young pickpocket who having quarrelled with his father, a Wesleyan minister: "determined to leave home, and nothing took away but what belonged to me. I had four sovereigns of pocket money and the suit of clothes I had on and a shirt. I walked to Shrewsbury and took the coach to London. When I first got to London I had neither friend nor acquaintance. I first put up in a coffee-shop in the Mile End Road and lodged there for seven weeks, till my money was nearly spent".

A mudlark, working in the Thames at Millwall, told Mayhew: "I was born in the county of Kerry in Ireland in the year 1847, and am now about thirteen years of age. My father was a ploughman and then lived on a farm in the service of a farmer, but now works at loading ships in the London Docks...My eldest brother is a seaman on board a screwship, now on a voyage to Hamburg; the other is a seaman now on his way to Naples".

Mayhew looked for down-and-outs or petty criminals to interview. Migrants were just as likely, however, to be skilled workers, like William Hart the cooper, or the Thompson brothers who arrived on the Island from Scotland in the 1850s. One of them had four children who included a boy named David. David grew up, went to work, married and settled on the Island. Amongst his children was a daughter, Sophie, born in 1879. Sophie lived to be over a hundred and a year or two before her death, she recorded her life story. Amongst her memories was her father's tale of the day the family first set foot on the Island.

"Do you remember the talk about the building of the *Great Eastern*, a boat called the *Great Eastern*, and when they launched it, it sunk? Well, my grandfather read in the daily paper in Scotland, first-class riveters wanted. well, my father was only six years old, so his father, uncle George and Jim and another of his brothers, there was my father's father and three of his brothers, all riveters, they couldn't get much work and they see this advert in the paper, they got their heads together and said, Well, what do you say, are you going to chance it? Yes, we'll have to sell up the bits of home and take what we can with us, take as much as we can with us but we'll have to make shift as long as we've got some bedclothes and clothes for the kids. Well, my father was the youngest, he was six years old, he came over. When they got over here, 'course, they'd got nowhere to go".

The family found an empty cottage by the river at a spot which later became Maconochie's factory. Here they settled down to their first night in their new home.

Alice Inkpen has traced the history of her family, the Bennetts, and discovered that her great-grand-father, Henry Bennet, was born in Mildenhall in Suffolk in 1816. Henry was the descendant of Hugenot farmers who had settled there in the 17th century, originally named "Bonnett" or "Bonnay". In 1851 he was living in King's Lynn with a young family. Twenty years later, he was on Millwall. His son, Charles Bennett, (Alice's grandfather) became a corn porter in the new Millwall Docks and married Hannah Burton, a maid in a Millwall hotel. Hannah came from Royston in Hertfordshire. They had nine children and lived in Janet Street.

The name Inkpen is a corruption of "Inger's Pen" a name dating back to pre-Norman times. Mrs Inkpen is not sure whether her husband's family originated from the village of Inkpen in Berkshire, though she has traced them back to the 1600s. There was a William in every generation and they were all artisans - decorators, plumbers and builders. Her husband's grandparents came to Cubitt Town from Lambeth in the middle of the 19th century, when it was first being developed by William Cubitt.

Although such precise records and memories

are rare, these stories of the origin of just three well-known Island families was repeated many times over in the middle of the 19th century. The pattern of many thousands of individual migrations is confirmed in statistics drawn from the census, taken every ten years since 1811 and, from 1841 onwards, showing the birthplace of every person recorded.

Thomas Cole (1981) analysed the birthplaces of household heads (usually married men) over the whole Isle of Dogs. He found that in 1851 roughly one quarter originated in Greater London and Middlesex. A slightly larger proportion came from east and south-east England, especially Kent, Essex and Surrey. About one-tenth came from the Midland counties, a somewhat smaller number from the west country, Wales and the border counties. 17% came from the northern counties, particularly Lancashire and Yorkshire, and from Scotland. A minority, 7.8%, came from Ireland.

Cole found that the more highly skilled migrants tended to be those who had travelled the greatest distance - like the Thompson brothers, who had riveting skills and who responded to an advertisement, confident that the efforts needed to make the long journey would be worth while. The Irish were the exception to this, being found almost universally amongst the labourers, though this may have been due to the prejudice they encountered in the labour market, rather than to any lack of skills on arrival here.

A study by the Island History Trust of the birthplaces of all the residents in Alfred Street in 1851 showed that over 50% were born in Poplar or other parts of London, reflecting the fact that there were 151 children under 12 in the street. The adults, over half of whom were aged between 30 and 50, came from London and from Kent, Surrey, Essex, the west country, the north, Scotland and Ireland in proportions similar to those recorded by Cole.

This regional mixture was to be found in all parts of the Island in the middle decades of the century, the period of its most rapid population growth, although Cole did find that there was some evidence that the Scots and Irish grouped together in the same streets. The former tended to be found in riverside cottages and along the southern part of West Ferry Road, while there was some gathering of the Scottish migrants around the Millwall shipyards where in fact the Thompson family found their empty cottage.

An observer of the time, Thomas Wright (1864) remarked on the mixture of regional accents he heard on the Island streets. He was particularly interested in the ship-building yards on Millwall where he noted that northern English and Scottish accents stood out.

"As I journeyed into the interior of the island the striking, distinctly-marked Scotch accent and phraseology continued to strike on my ear at almost every step; for owing to the sharp ringing noise caused by the riveting hammers which are at work in all parts of the island for many hours in the day, the inhabitants acquire a habit of speaking very loud when in the streets. And thus the broadly-accented "How are ye?" and the "Brawly, how are ye?" which the gude wives exchange when they meet, and the invitations to come awa' in (to the public house) and have "twa pennyworth" or "a wee drap dram", reach my ears. During meal hours and the early part of the evening, when the workmen are passing through the streets, the ascendancy of the Scottish tongue is still more apparent..."

Wright distinguished between the "dry humourous Scotchmen" (who included the Thompson brothers) and the "burly Lancashire men...as good tempered as they are big"...and the "dapper, sprightly Cockneys" who made up some of the population and so he gives us a glimpse of the blend of regional accents which made up the sound of the Island at this time. A babble of different voices resounded in the streets, the pubs, the shops, the first schools and churches and in the workplace.

As well as the strong northern accents and the cockney's London twang, there were the drawn-out vowels of East Anglia and the burr of the west country, the lilting tones of the Welsh and the clipped nasal sound of the Midlands. Many curious words would have been heard and at times it would have been hard to understand each other's accents.

Along with these regional variations in language went other differences. Their outlook on life, and the knowledge they carried with them, varied according to their age, their origins and their experience

There were distinctive styles of dress - most people wore boots or shoes made by a local cobbler and clothes which were home-made or locally produced in a local style, some indicating a particular trade, like the farrier's leather apron. They came from independent, isolated mining settlements, from rural villages under the control of a great landowner, from fishing villages and forest hamlets. They brought with them different moral codes, work-place practices, domestic habits, songs, stories, childhood games, favourite sports and religious beliefs. They brought the wisdom to forecast the weather, to handle horses, to brew beer, to make tallow dips, to spin and weave, to identify the tree from which timber had come, to attend at childbirth and to lay out a corpse, to recite the Psalms, to grow vegetables, raise animals for food, bake lardy cakes and Cornish pasties, set broken bones and use wild herbs as medicine. They included peaceful Quakers, tight-lipped Wesleyans, strict Presbyterians, drinkers, abstainers, the meek and the assertive, the clever and the slow-witted, the political and the indifferent, the rational and the superstitious, those clinging to old ideas and those eager for the new.

As well as encompassing so many regional differences, the new industrial population of the Island was also a mixture of all the social classes - only the aristocracy was missing.

One of the changes which happened as part of the Industrial Revolution, and which also took many decades to complete, was that people began to live in different areas according to their social class. In the early stages of industrial development on the Isle of Dogs, that separation was not yet evident, though it was becoming so by the 1860s. We saw earlier how local employers like Pitcher and Napier had their own houses on the Island close to their place of business, in line with traditional, pre-industrial practice.

Cole (1981) found that a small but significant number of heads of households living on the Island in 1841 were in the highest social class of large employers, which included shipbuilders and manufacturers. This group broadened out as the century progressed to encompass bankers, estate agents, doctors and clerics, who, he said, were less wealthy but "very affluent by local standards and enjoyed considerable local prestige." The families in this group employed servants and lived in their own villas or in the biggest of the houses built in Millwall and Cubitt Town, in Ord Street, Wharf Road and West Ferry Road.

In the middle class were men (and some women) who owned smaller businesses or managed a business for someone else, as well as shop-keepers and publicans, public officials and professionals such as teachers. They also lived at their place of business or in the bigger, bay-windowed houses on the main roads or residential side streets, and employed one or more servants. This group included people like Charles Davis, the landlord of the *Manchester*

Arms and of several houses in Cubitt Town; William Roberts, maker of fire engines, who lived in West Ferry Road and employed 22 men and two boys.

The largest occupational group were men in skilled and semi-skilled work. This group grew from 37.5% to over 50% of the total population of household heads between 1831 and 1861, reflecting the nature and prosperity of the local economy. Half of them worked in ship-building, engineering and the metal trades, and the Thompson brothers, who were taken on as riveters on the *Great Eastern*, were in this group; others were coopers, lightermen, watermen, ropemakers and brick-makers (the last-named group was associated with the development of Cubitt Town which was completed in the 1860s). Because living space was in short supply, the families in this group lived all over the Island without any noticeable separation from the poorest group, the unskilled labourers. These made up between one quarter and one-third of the population between 1831 and 1861 and Cole noted that they were quite likely to live in the oldest cottages by the riverside and along West Ferry Road.

If we turn again to our detailed study of Alfred Street in 1851, occupations recorded in the census reflect this Island-wide mixture of skilled, semi-skilled and labouring household heads. There was one public official, a Customs officer, who might be regarded as middle-class. There were 14 men who worked on the river, 42 who worked in ship-building, engineering and the metal trades, 12 skilled in the building trades, and 11 with miscellaneous skills such as "ivory turner" and "practical chemist". (This last group includes two miners, puzzling until we see that they must have been very recent arrivals, as one of them had a young daughter born in Yorkshire). Nine individuals were engaged in small-scale trade, such as butcher, milkman, coal dealer etc. Alongside these 89 men with clearly defined trades or occupations were 52 "labourers", nine apprentices and two errand boys. 12 women recorded an occupation: five were engaged in laundry work, one was a needlewoman, three were domestic servants, one a watercress seller, one a nurse and one a "leadworker, labourer".

Millwall Dock Company directors, contractors and engineers on a visit to the docks under construction, with their families. 1860s.

This detailed study bears out the results of Cole's broader-based research, showing a higher proportion of skilled workers than labourers in the population as a whole, though the latter were still well represented, and with perhaps just "a touch of class" in the Customs Officer, who could be regarded as "professional" or "white collar".

A sense of this mixed society, where on certain occasions all social classes mingled freely, is found in press reports of the launching of the *Great Eastern* on Millwall in 1858. *The Illustrated Times* described the scene, when the Island was dressed up as for a festival"

"Across the narrow streets, from public-house to public-house, were stretched broad flowing flags and every apartment in every house, if it commanded a view of the great vessel, was turned 'inside out' to accommodate visitors. Bands of music were enlivening the scene at the various public houses, even at the early hour of ten in the morning."

On the river itself, as well as upon the opposite shore, were yet more scenes of wild enthusiasm:

"Surely the water was never more darkened before, with such a mass of noisy, crowding, pushing people, acting upon the treacherous element as if they were at the doors of a theatre. Across the water upon the wharves and houses the land is alive with spectators, who are heaving and shouting, while the church bells ring, the bands play and the flags wave...At a rough computation, there cannot be less than 100,000 persons present on this day at one o'clock."

The crowd included: "Beggars, mountebanks, musicians, street tumblers, men with wooden legs, vocalists, pickpockets, bankers, merchants, ambassadors, Punch and Judy men, members of Parliament, lords and ladies, mechanics, reporters, engineers, quidnuncs, idlers, literati, swell mobsters, dignitaries of the church, old women, young girls, Lascars, Chinese, Malays, Frenchmen, Irishmen...."

And amongst them were the Thompson brothers and their families, now settled in their new Island home and eagerly waiting to see the results of their labours as the great ship was launched into the Thames.

6. Aspects of Everyday Life

The mixture of social classes found on the Island in the early period of industrialisation did not mean that there were no social barriers. The reverse was true. The wealthy, marked by their clean, expensive and well cut clothes and a general air of being well-fed, were able to shut themselves off in their private carriages and comfortable homes, even when these were close to their business premises. Their common interests united them as they met at private dinners and as subscribers or members of local organisations for safeguarding their interests. They had shared investments and family connections. Jabez Binks, of the Millwall wire rope works, married the "beautiful and talented" Mary Bellamy, daughter of Edward Bellamy of Millwall Tank Works, in 1859, thus uniting two families with similar business interests. This was only one of many similarly suitable matches.

Until the Second Reform Act of 1867 extended the franchise to working men, employers and landlords controlled local politics and public affairs, as Members of Parliament and through the local Board of Works, Board of Guardians and other similar organisations.

We have already seen how local businessmen had invested in West Ferry Road in 1812. There was an equally strong local presence amongst the commissioners of Sewers for Poplar Marsh. In 1833 they included John Garford, a magistrate of Poplar, commemorated in the street of that name; Richard and Henry Green, the Blackwall shipbuilders whose father, George, founded a local school, William Fearnall, shipbuilder, of Fletcher Son & Fearnall; Charles Price, oil and candle merchant, William Mellish, landowner and grazier; Samuel Brown, chain maker; William Tooke MP, Sir John Woolmore, Henry Loftus Wigram, shipbuilder and William Curling who had a shipyard at Limehouse Hole.

Local businessmen were also to be found in the Millwall Literary Society, the Millwall Committee and the Isle of Dogs Improvement Society, the latter an unsuccessful attempt, led by William Cubitt, to establish the Island as a separate administrative parish.

Cowper records the Island's first full-time, purpose-built school, opened in 1847. In 1846 the government had introduced measures to provide a minimum education for poor children in charity schools. The pupil-teacher system was introduced and grants were made available to philanthropic organisations like the British and Foreign Schools Society. British Street School on Millwall, which later evolved into Harbinger School, was one of the results. Cowper noted

of Glengall, whilst William Cubitt bore the brunt of the building costs, and all the largest local employers were on the list of founding subscribers.

When St. Luke's church was first formed as a seprate congregation in 1863, land for the new building was donated by Lady Margaret Charteris (daughter of the Countess of Glengall). Local businessmen who played a significant role in funding and supporting the new church included Richard Watkins, Esquire, of Millwall, of the firm Jackson and Watkins, shipbuilders and engineers, and J and A Fuller, barge builders. The church was used as a day school until a purpose-built school was erected in 1871. The land was given by the Earl of Strafford and local businessmen were amongst the Trustees.

The Methodist church in Cubitt Town also had the support of wealthy benefactors. In 1858 John Crosby moved to the Island from Poplar and finding fellow Methodists amongst his associates, set up a meeting room in his home at 20 Davis Terrace, Manchester Road. Within two years the congregation had outgrown its space and appeals were made to the landlord, Charles Davis, for permission to make two rooms into one. This was refused - perhaps because Mr Davis was also the landlord of *The Manchester Arms* and did not share the temperance views of the Methodists.

John Crosby's wife, Eliza, was the sister of Joseph Westwood of the Cubitt Town shipbuilders Westwood Baillie & Co., and he helped the Methodists to obtain a lease on a site for a new chapel in Manchester Road. His son, Joseph Westwood junior, (who later founded the firm of Westwood and Company) laid the foundation stone in July 1862 at a ceremony followed by a public tea. Amongst the donors to

that : "The management is in the hands of a committee of ladies and a committee of gentlemen."

In 1855 a group of local ship-builders and bankers founded Poplar Hospital as a place to which workers who had suffered accidents in the local docks and factories could be taken for speedy medical assistance. The list of subscribers who paid their supporting guineas to the hospital fund in the mid-1860s included many Island industrialists and landowners.

The Island's first place of worship, a Congregational chapel which may also have included a day school, was founded in West Ferry Road by local businessman James Grellier in 1817.

Island businessmen and landowners were involved in founding the Island's first Anglican church, Christ Church, consecrated in 1857. The land was donated by the Countess the building fund was Sir William Cubitt.

Another founder of Cubitt Town Methodist Chapel was Henry Barcham, grocer, of Manchester Road. Henry was born in Sheringham in Norfolk in 1846 and was a blacksmith by trade. His father Robert had also been a blacksmith in Sheringham, and their ancestors were farmers and sailors. His involvement with the Cubitt Town Methodists was a continuation of his family's long involvement with the Methodist Church in Sheringham.

The founding of churches and schools was not the end of the involvement of the Island's middle class in its affairs, as in most cases they continued to make donations and to serve on governing bodies. The women in their families were active in fund-raising, visiting schools and finding places in service for those Island girls they considered sufficiently respectable.

Middle- and upper-class interest in the moral and social welfare of the working-classes was not purely philanthropic. Everyday life during much of the 19th century was characterised by extremes of poverty and injustice and by public and private violence. The politics of the period were such that conflict between employers and workers was constantly erupting or threatened. In their role as magistrates and justices of the peace employers were able to implement the laws and administer the punishments designed to keep rebellion at bay. John Stewart enlisted dozens of his workmen as special constables, willing or not, during the Chartist agitation of the 1840s. It was also well understood by the employing class that a docile and industrious workforce, instructed in the classic mid-Victorian values of thrift, civic obedience and self-help, was very much to their advantage. Schools and churches were important channels for communicating those values.

The provision of social benefits in the work place was rare - canteens, first-aid, sick pay, etc., were all unheard of, though in the heady days of the early 1860s one Millwall employer did splash out on his workmen. At his Blackwall yard, C.J. Mare had been noted as a bad payer of wages, often spending the money at the races instead. However his Millwall Iron Works appear to have been exemplary in providing ideal conditions for the time, with spacious dining hall, large stove and reading room, where the employees could run their rowing club, cricket club and band.

Working people themselves helped to set up churches and schools. Many also believed it would be better for them to engage directly in the political life of the country rather than wait for the wealthy to hand out benefits, and took part in campaigns to extend the vote and improve working conditions. They had independent forms of self-help organisation in the work place and their own meeting places in the public houses.

The first Roman Catholic church of St. Edwards was established in Moiety Street in 1846 to serve the Irish Catholic community but it lacked wealthy supporters and fell into a ruinous state before a new church, St. Edmund's, was built in 1876. St. Edward's was also a day school. The Scottish Presbyterians, who were among those who came from the north to work

St. Edward's Chapel and Schools, mid 19th century

in the Millwall shipyards, built their own church, St. Paul's, later always referred to as "The Scotch Church", in West Ferry Road, in the 1850s. They had financial help from John Scott Russell in this enterprise but are believed to have done much of the building work themselves. (The foundation stones and interior roof trusses of the church, now The Space Art Centre, still evoke the presence of the Presbyterian shipwrights). Mrs Sophie Anderson, descendant of the Thompson family, attended the Scotch Church regularly.

Wesleyan Methodism also came to Millwall in the shape of four young shipwrights - James Barron and his friends Harlow, Ward and Spencer - all staunch Wesleyans and employed in Carter's Dock. As the nearest chapel was at

Limehouse they decided to set up their own society and rented an old marine store for the purpose. By the end of 1846 they had 67 scholars enrolled in the Sunday School.

Their Christian beliefs aside, working men and their wives knew the value of the basic literacy skills which could be learnt in the Sunday School and through even a short period of attendance at the day schools commonly attached to their churches. Limited government grants were available for building schools and Christ Church had a school in Billson Street. The first St. Luke's Church, known as the "Iron Church" and built in the 1860s, was used as a day school and had 200 children on its books in 1866; St. Edwards, the first Roman Catholic church, was also used as a day school and there were also a few individuals who set up private schools in their own homes.

But in the middle of the 19th century, education for all was still only a pipe dream. There was little time or opportunity to learn, since school places were limited and cost valuable pennies. Most children of working-class families were expected to start contributing to the family income as soon as they were able. For girls who were not kept at home to help, this might mean becoming nursemaids, cleaners, or doing needlework. Prostitution was the resource of the most desperate, like Mayhew's dock labourer's daughter. For boys and young men, there was plenty of opportunity to become apprentices and labourers in the ship yards and iron works.

David Thompson was only six when he arrived on Millwall in 1857 but his brothers were already old enough to work: "They could take the hot rivets from the furnace to where the worker was working; they didn't ask the age then, they was big boys, they was all right. It was only years later when all these rules come out you had to be a certain age for this and a certain age for that".

Skilled workers attached a great deal of importance to their membership of local benefit or friendly societies, which protected them from the initial shocks of unemployment, illness and bereavement. William Hart, the cooper who worked for 33 years at the West India Docks, belonged to a trade organisation, even though trade unions were officially banned until 1824 under the Combination Acts, passed in the 1790s by an anxious government.

The shipwrights were noted among the London trades for the strength and resilience of their societies. They were amongst the highest paid of craftsmen when in work, which gave them the resources to be self-supporting for short periods of unemployment. They also enforced various measures to restrict entry to their craft and thus protect their livelihoods. Associated trades with the same status included those of mast makers, sail makers, riggers, rope makers and caulkers. Availability of work varied with the season and according to the skills or traditions associated with particular yards, and with the state of a particular export trade.

Admission to the trade of shipwright was through a seven year apprenticeship. Shipwrights worked in gangs, ranging in number from as few as four to as many as thirty, each gang having a leader. Such gangs might last for years, or be

Building and repairing wooden ships, c.1843

brought together for a specific job. Shipwrights owned their own tools, were not tied to any particular employer, negotiated contracts for each job through their foreman or leading hand, frequently had Saturday as well as Sunday off.

London shipwrights, like all working men, did not have the vote and they expressed their political will either through trade union activity or in direct action. In 1820 Queen Caroline of Brunswick came home to take the throne beside her husband, now George IV. He, however, wished to divorce her on grounds of adultery (disregarding his own series of mistresses). London working people of all trades seized her cause as their own, and the shipwrights and other shipbuilding trades of London were in the forefront of a campaign to protect her.

On one occasion three thousand shipwrights and caulkers assembled in Stepney, of which the Isle of Dogs is part, and proceeded on foot to present an address to the Queen at her house.

Queen Caroline

Contemporary descriptions of the event give some sense of the strength and the prosperity of their organisation. The procession was led by two men on white horses and included numerous silk banners and flags, models of ships in every stage of building, and four bands. The men marched six abreast, were "very clean and respectable in appearance" and all wore sprigs of oak or laurel, or white favours.

Processions, whether strictly organised and "respectable", violent and unruly, whether political, topical or religious in intent, were one of the most important ways open to working people to express their ideals and beliefs throughout the century. The mass demonstrations by supporters of the Charter in the 1830s and 1840s are a further reminder of this, and they are echoed in the dignified marches of the striking port workers much later in the century. Processions could have a cultural meaning too. Cole says of the Irish parades on the Island: "Hundreds participated...bands played Irish folk songs; and large, silk banners with the harp of Erin and wreaths of shamrocks in the centre...surrounded by the motto "God Save Ireland" left no doubt as to the identity and loyalty of the marchers."

East London was one of the centres of Chartist organisation and agitation in the 1830s and 1840s. The East London Democratic Federation had its headquarters in the Minories.

William Lovett was the General Convention member for "London and its districts" but Tower Hamlets had its own representative in Robert Hartwell. Chartists were united in their aims for annual parliaments, universal male suffrage and the secret ballot, but were divided as to the right tactics to achieve these, some favouring direct and militant action, others confident that mass petitions would win the day. London had supporters of both camps - a cache of arms was found in the Trades Hall in Bethnal Green in 1840, "and the police were put on the alert for fear of an insurrection". (Palmer) The Royal Horse Guards were brought to Victoria Park when a demonstration was planned at Bonners Fields in 1848.

The Chartists did not win any of their six points and the movement slowly fell apart in the face of imprisonments, the violent breaking-up of demonstrations, and slowly rising wages. Some Chartists emigrated and took their beliefs with them to America, Australia and New Zealand. Others became active in the emerging co-operative and trade union movements.

Many supporters of the Chartist movement had been workers whose traditional skills were becoming redundant. With the arrival of mechanisation, new groups of workers, such as engineers, were becoming more numerous and more powerful. On the Island, with the coming of steam power, the flow of shipping into the port became more regular and also increased in volume, whilst working practices changed and new skills were acquired. The relatively leisurely pace of production in the yards building wooden ships gave way to the mastery of steam and iron, noisier, dirtier, heavier and above all faster than traditional methods. Accurate measurements became essential and the old ways of measuring by eye had to be given up. New skills in mechanical and constructional engineering had to be learned.

The most significant development in working class politics in mid-century was the growth of what came to be known as "new model" unions. Formed out of the existing networks of localised unions amongst skilled trades, these emerged in the 1850s as national organisations, with full-time paid staff. One of the most prominent of these new unions was the Amalgamated Society of Engineers, which by 1850 had a membership of 11,000, mostly in London and in Lancashire. During the 1860s the trade unions and the trades councils drew on their new-found strength as well as their Chartist heritage to campaign successfully for political change. The Reform Act of 1867, though it fell far short of the ideals of chartism, gave the urban working man the vote for the first time.

A journalist wrote of the Island in mid-century that it was : "a large, thriving, populous town...There are factories and workshops, and hundreds of businesses connected with the seas and navigation, already extending round its banks, a perfect cordon girdling it."

The size of the workforce in some of the new yards was breathtaking. Thousands of workers were employed at peak periods. Fairbairn's yard employed up to 2,000 hands at full capacity in the 1840s. 1,500 men and boys worked at Russell's yard in the 1850s and when this became The Millwall Ironworks in the 1860s, between four and five thousand men and boys were said to be employed there. Samuda's yard in Cubitt Town had work for two thousand and John Dudgeon, who owned an engine works on Millwall and a shipyard in Cubitt Town, employed 650 at the former and 850 at the latter. Island yards were renowned for their size, for the quality of their products and for their advanced technology, and it was a matter of

Casting a cylinder at John Scott Russell's Shipyard, Isle of Dogs, 1854

pride to be employed there.

Living standards varied considerably within the Island's labour force. There were skilled craftsmen, semi-skilled operators of machinery, unskilled labourers; there were shipwrights, engineers, apprentices, casual labourers; stevedores and dockers, grain porters and barrow boys. Ship-yard labourers earned more than factory workers, dock and wharf labourers still less, being amongst the lowest paid at between nine and fourteen shillings a week. Stevedores, shipworkers and specialist handlers of grain and timber earned more than those employed as casual dockers. The workers classed as semi-skilled and the labourers had less freedom of movement than the skilled men, and were more likely to stay put in a familiar place than to move away in search of work. They were also unlikely to belong to trade unions or friendly societies, and so more likely to slide rapidly into poverty when no work was available.

In the comparatively secure economic climate of the 1850s, the new unions were soon powerful enough to command shorter working hours and better wages in certain trades. Blacksmiths, engineers, boiler makers and riveters, like the 22 men employed by William Roberts, and the Thompson brothers, and skilled men in the building trades, earned anything from thirty-two to forty-two shillings a week. Shipwrights earned over forty shillings a week and caulkers and riggers were also well paid. Mrs Anderson said that when her grandfather and his two brothers were taken on as riveters in Scott Russell's yard in the 1850s, they: "earned tons of money and of course they all got on".

Wages still went up and down according to local custom, piece work, and special contracts, but an old caulker recalled in 1908 that in the middle of the 19th century the Isle of Dogs had been: "...a gold mine...Shipyards had keels on every slip...The old City Canal was full of craft. The docks were full of ships loading and unloading and discharging and others waiting for their berths and more ships being built all around you...even a man of seventy-five could get a job then..." (*East End News* London 29th August 1908, quoted in Cole) Such high wages amongst such large numbers of skilled workers created a group which could afford to eat well, maintain comfortable homes, pay their friendly society dues, indulge in boat-racing, in boxing and other athletic sports, give their children what ever education was available and in general maintain a living standard which clearly distinguished them

as a confident, prosperous aristocracy of labour on the Isle of Dogs. Thomas Wright said of the skilled workers on the Island: "there is a certain understood dignity and exclusiveness of caste pertaining to the artisan class that every individual of it is practically compelled to respect and support."

The story of the Thompson brothers shows that skilled workers ate well and easily got credit Mrs Anderson related how on arrival the family found an empty cottage and slept the night there. The next morning they went out and found a butcher's shop open, Baileys. After he heard their story, the butcher gave them a big jug of hot tea and told them to come back and see him at dinner time. The men were taken on immediately at Scott Russell's yard and went back to see the butcher later that day: "Went back and told Mr Bailey at the butcher's shop, and he said, That's good news, now what you want to eat, come to me, and when you get your wages you can pay me back, you can have whatever you want".

Mrs Anderson added that when this butcher opened his shop in the morning he had a hundred pieces of steak in the window and they were all gone by dinner time. Thomas Wright described the street sellers with hot coffee and baked potatoes just before six o'clock, the breakfast relishes of herrings, watercress, shrimps or whatever was in season, on sale at half past eight and the good breakfast of coffee, bread and butter and an egg, which "can be got here for fourpence halfpenny".

Beer was cheap, spirits comparatively so, and drunkenness was commonplace, though perhaps not as excessive as the reports of the temperance reformers claimed. Public houses were important centres for meeting and entertainment, as well as for quenching thirst. There were many of them on the Isle of Dogs, some very large. In 1853 Cowper listed "ten houses licensed for the sale of wines, spirits, etc., these being, in order from the north end of West Ferry Road: *City Arms, Anchor and Hope, Torrington Arms, Tooke Arms, Kings Arms, Glengall Arms, Robert Burns, Ferry House, Newcastle Arms* and *Folly House*. All but the *Ferry House* and the *Folly House* were new. There were a number of beer shops on Millwall and several more pubs were added when Cubitt Town was developed - *The Pier*, the *George Hotel*, the *Cubitt Arms*, *The Dorset*, the *London Tavern*, *The Queen* and the *Manchester Arms*. The big rooms on the first floor of the larger pubs were used for concerts or variety shows until mid-century licensing laws forced these early "music halls" out of the pubs and into purpose built theatres such as *The Queen's* in Poplar High Street.

Public houses had their own clientele, in the early days often organised around ethnic origin - the Scots and Irish favouring their own - or else around particular trades. Pubs also served as meeting places for trade unions, friendly societies and other groups including "Judge and Jury" clubs. Indoor games were played there and music and singing were enjoyed; gambling was carried on. Sporting events like illegal cock-fighting, dog-fights and bare-fist fights, as well as athletics, cricket and football matches, swimming challenges and races on the river, were arranged in pubs.

The arrival of formally organised sport helped to keep lads off the street, where they were a potential nuisance. Referring to this universal problem on the Island, Wright described the boys and apprentices he saw hanging about as: "great in the performance of intricate shuffles and break-down dances and are noted for the early acquirement and energetic singing of the popular songs of the hour". They also operated a protection racket "Give us something to leave you alone", they would say to the proprietor of a stall and if he is wise he does not refuse. It may be asked, why not set the police upon these young scamps?...In the course of my visits to the island I have seen divers street and public-house rows but I have never seen a policeman."

The games and pastimes of the boys and apprentices were often informal training grounds for more serious participation in competitive sports. Boxing and athletics had long been popular , with big events often staged to coincide with the great annual fairs like the one at Greenwich. As these fairs died away or changed to become more controlled and less boisterous, dedicated arenas such as the Prince of Wales' Running Ground, at Bow, made their appearance. Bare-fist scuffles on the street led on to membership of a boxing club, knocking balls about was practise for cricket or football games - there were organised cricket clubs in the East End by the 1860s. Swimming and rowing were encouraged by the closeness of the river, in spite of the dangers, and Poplar and Blackwall Rowing Club was established in 1860, with many watermen and lightermen amongst its members.

When the big crash came in 1866 and a number of Island shipyards closed down overnight, many other companies which supplied the yards also shut down. For the shipyards, this was not a temporary depression. The great days of ship-building on the Thames had come to an end. The immediate result was massive unemployment amongst all sections of the thousands-strong workforce which had been employed in the yards and associated industries. Many skilled workers returned to their former homes in the north of England and in Scotland where ship-building and coal and iron production was expanding - though the Thompson brothers stayed.

The *Eastern Daily Post*, reporting conditions on Millwall in December 1868, said there were upwards of 6,000 people in receipt of the workhouse dole where three years previously there had been hardly 600. The paper described the community of men, women and children as foodless, fireless, half-clad and hopeless and called on the "never-failing charity of England" to put matters right in advance of Government legislation to equalise the poor rates and provide a more generous system of relief. In February 1869 the *Dorset County Chronicle and Somersetshire Gazette* reported details of the death through starvation of a mother and child on Millwall. The husband "had since become insane".

Shopkeepers, publicans and other small businesses all felt the pinch. It was reported in the press that a butcher on Millwall had difficulty in selling even a bit of bullock's liver to his poverty-stricken customers. A woman who ran a coffee shop not far from the Millwall Iron Works described how all her savings had gone and she had sold her horse and trap, her husband's watch, some rings and other articles of jewellery in order to feed her family. Her son, who was the proprietor of two nearby shops, had shut them up and "tramped it" to Southampton, where he was obliged to accept a situation as stoker on board a steamer. The public houses, which had formerly done "an immense trade" now scarcely sold twenty gallons of beer in a week. Amongst the rich, private carriages had to be given up as a result of the financial crisis, hard luck for their former owners, even worse for the farriers, coach builders, grooms, chandlers and saddlers who were put out of work as a result.

This financial crisis hit Thames ship-builders hard and altered the fortunes of share-holders in the Millwall Dock and Canal Company. But the crisis was short-lived. The British economy was still expanding and before long investors were contemplating new developments on the Isle of Dogs, drawn there by its empty riverside sites and its skilled, under-employed workforce.

The Second Industrial Phase - 1860s to 1914

7. Introduction

When the Horseshoe Company in Cubitt Town lost a big order to the Americans in 1907 it was a disaster for the company and evidence of the general trend of increasing competition for British industry from both the United States and Europe, especially Germany. During the last quarter of the 19th century the manufacturing sector of the British economy lost its early monopoly and had to face rivalry from the newly industrialised nations. These years were also a time of further discoveries and inventions, and of the rise of organised labour.

British reserves of coal and iron continued to be extracted and used in manufacturing; steam engines were being applied more and more to industrial production. Steel replaced iron as a more malleable and longer-lasting material for construction and manufacture. Towards the end of the period, the power of electricity was harnesed. Railways and rolling stock built in Britain, and iron bridges built on the Isle of Dogs, were being exported round the world, together with skilled engineers.

The railways opened up the interiors of America, Canada, Russia, India, Africa and South America. British steamships carried goods and people round the globe. River boats were built by Yarrows on the Thames and in other shipyards to be used in the exploration of the dense forests and vast plains of the great continents. In this and other ways British influence extended to larger areas of the world. Britain bought the Suez Canal in 1875, improving trade routes for steam ships. Large areas of East and West Africa were brought under British control on the laudable pretext of suppressing the slave trade which had traditionally thrived there.

As the railway, the steamship and the electric telegraph linked the nations of the world in a trading network, rich natural resources of timber, metals, petroleum, chemicals and foodstuffs were discovered and exploited by the Europeans, whilst the non-industrialised countries became expanding new markets for their manufactured products. London's role as an international financial centre was enhanced by millions of pounds of new investment flowing through the Stock Exchange.

There was intense competition between the industrial nations for control of these resources and markets, competition which led to many minor skirmishes and which was a major contributory cause of the First World War. In Britain the idea of "Empire" was most evident in popular culture in the decades leading up to the turn of the century, partly in response to the perceived threat of other industrial states, particularly Germany.

The continued expansion of the manufacturing and processing sectors of the British economy fed the growth of great sprawling urban centres. The population of London was five times greater at the end of Victoria's reign than it had been when she came to the throne. This growth of towns and cities was marked by increasing physical separation between the social classes. Once the relationship between bad hygiene, poor sanitation and infectious diseases had been acknowledged, the rich created their own exclusive suburbs and country retreats, well away from the smoky, smelly sources of their wealth. Their private carriages, first-class rail travel and by 1900, their motor cars, insulated them from the mass of the people and gave them easy access to city centres and seaside watering-places.

For the growing middle-class of lawyers, accountants, doctors and other professionals, the owners of small business, managers and white collar workers, a house-building boom created streets and suburbs of villas and substantial terraces, still visible and in use all over Britain. Tramcars and omnibuses ferried them to and fro between work and home.

The working classes crowded into the inner-city homes abandoned by the rich, into hastily erected terraces and tenements, into old cottages and new Peabody Buildings.

The "Hungry Forties" were gone. Wages rose between the 1850s and 1900 and falling food prices made it possible for urban working people to eat regularly and adequately. This was due partly to the booming economy and partly to bulk imports of grain, meat and fruit from Australia, Canada, New Zealand and Africa. Cheap food supplies from abroad had a downside for agricultural workers and farmers. Many farms were sold up or absorbed into larger units during the 1870s and 1880s. At the same time, local handicraft industries, such as furniture making, or

Yarrow's shipbuilding yard, Cubitt Town, about 1900, showing the construction of destroyer and torpedo boats for the Japanese government.

straw-hat making, were being mechanised and moved to urban centres. The exodus from the land, which we have seen going on for some time, accelerated.

The greater exodus was still in progress - the migratory movement of thousands of people from Europe to America and from Britain to the colonies. Many European migrants passed through London on their way to Liverpool, and some settled here, like the Russian Jews in Whitechapel.

As well as cheaper and more varied food, other products were appearing which altered lifestyles. They included the camera, the combustion engine, the bicycle, antiseptic, anaesthetic, linoleum, electric light and power, canned food and refrigeration, the telephone and the typewriter.

The benefits of these new products were not for everyone. In living standards, the gap between rich and poor widened. Poorly paid domestic servants, the majority of them women and girls, laboured in the homes of the rich to keep fires burning, enormous meals on the table and clean linen on the beds. The lush Victorian interiors of well-to-do homes, even amongst the lower middle-class, contrasted sharply with the plain furniture and rag rugs of working class homes, where the hard labour of scrubbing and washing and cooking fell to the women of the family, some of whom were also wage-earners. Thousands of needlewomen damaged their eyesight by sewing into the night to make the elaborate silk dresses worn by wealthy women, while many working class mothers had a new apron once a year as a sole addition to their wardrobe.

A number of middle-class people tried to cross this divide through voluntary work amongst the poor, some even settling down to live amongst those they wished to help. Members of the temperance movement tried to draw people away from the temporary solace of the public house, and charitable workers laboured to raise standards of hygiene and domestic economy in homes which in many cases had no running water or regular income.

In the workplace, conditions were harsh. The pressure of foreign competition led manufacturers to try to speed up the production process, by using new forms of lighting and power to lengthen the working day and to bring machinery into manufacturing. This also led to de-skilling and the introduction of cheap juvenile labour into the workshop. In some sectors, it meant continued and growing reliance on an army of cheap labour, drawn on as required, abandoned when no longer needed. The deep divide between rich and poor in terms of living standards was reflected in the way in which employers, with a few notable exceptions, treated their workers as practically sub-human, denying them basic amenities such as fresh drinking water, washrooms, toilets, restrooms and canteens, and providing no safety measures to protect them against machinery, heat, dust, chemicals and noxious fumes.

Politically this period was marked by the extension of the vote to adult men and the rise of the organised labour movement. The "new model unions" of skilled men which developed in the 1850s sought to improve wages and working conditions, both by making their own provisions and through alliances with the existing political parties, particularly the Liberals. Dissatisfaction with the results of this strategy and the influence of European politics contributed to the growth of a more broad-based socialist movement, encompassing a variety of idealisms - Christian Socialism, anarchism, communism, syndicalism. In the 1880s unskilled workers successfully formed unions, and by the 1890s, the stage was set for the appearance of the Independent Labour Party and the weakening of the link between the Liberal Party and the unions. The Parliamentary Labour Party was formed in 1906. At the same time, the women's suffrage movement was gathering strength.

Between the turn of the century and the First World War, wages fell in relation to food prices. Since working people had by then come to expect a certain living standard, if an insecure and relatively poor one, and were even becoming ambitious for rather more than existence on the poverty line, this was a period of social unrest marked by riots and strikes in various parts of the country. In London's docks, "tension between management and men was as dramatic and persistent as it had ever been" (Pudney).

Another distinctive feature of this period from the 1860s to the First World War was the increasing role of the state in everyday life. This already existed at its most draconian in the form of the Poor Law. New legislation, intended for the betterment of the working class, was made by a Parliament still dominated by the ruling class and indifferent to the fresh burdens they were imposing. The growth of the state is most obvious in the provision of a basic education for working-class children - who were obliged to attend school from the 1880s onwards. Parents were drawn into a bureacratic structure which involved inspectors calling, payment of fines, and later, medical inspections and assessment for free school meals. The requirement for midwives to register in order to practice reduced the number of able and familiar women who could attend at births. There was, however, a general welcome for the Old Age Pensions Act of 1908.

8. The Industrial Island

The great years of Thames ship-building ended in the 1860s and a new phase in the economy of the Isle of Dogs began, a phase of intense industrial activity which was to last for the next hundred years.

In this period the dock companies suffered various changes of fortune as the success of the early docks promoted further growth.

The construction of the West India and London Docks was swiftly followed by the Surrey Commercial Docks south of the river. In 1838, the East and West India Dock Company was formed out of two long-standing rivals. The Royal Albert and Victoria Docks were built in mid-century, and the Millwall Docks were opened on the Isle of Dogs in 1868. In the same year, the former City Canal, which had already been partly enlarged, was widened along its entire length to become the New South Dock, making the third of the three West India Dock Basins. Twenty years later came Tilbury Dock.

Rivalry between the dock companies reached new heights as each successive dock was opened, each new dock being further down-river and with more modern accommodation, than its predecessors. Rate-cutting to attract business was mutually destructive in the long term, since it left companies with insufficient investment capital. In 1900 a Royal Commission was appointed to look into the future of the London Docks, faced as they were with competition from other ports. Its report in 1902 recommended a new central authority, which eventually materialised in 1909 as the Port of London Authority.

One outcome of the fierce competition between the private companies was the progressive casualisation and impoverishment of the port workers, particularly the dockers and stevedores. However the docks always provided work, or the possibility of work, for many different grades of worker - casual labourer, semi-skilled, clerical and master tradesmen.

The docks also stimulated demand for local products like packagings and ropes and for services such as storage and transport. The ship-repair industry was kept busy working on the vessels which used the Port and alongside this, makers of small boats and barges continued to thrive. Complementing these industries were marine, civil and mechanical engineering works, some of which had grown from small beginnings out of the legacy of the inventors and ship-builders of the early 19th century.

The larger engineering firms undertook contracts in distant parts of the world, erecting gas holders, building bridges, replacing engine parts, repairing ships in dry dock; gangs of men went from the Island to the coast of Africa to mend the boilers of a broken-down tanker, and into the English countryside to build gas holders at the edge of a town. Many Island names became known throughout the UK and world-wide as a result of this.

Among the famous firms associated with the Island in this period were Brown Lenox and Company the chain cable makers, Joseph Westwoods, electrical and mechanical engineers, Matthew T.Shaw, constructional engineers, Thomas Tierney, Cargo Fleet Iron Company, constructional engineers, Locke Lancaster & Company, lead processors, Le Bas Tubes, manufacturers of tubes and fittings, Samuel Cutler, constructional engineers, Rye Arc Welding, Badcocks the barge builders, Hawkins & Tipson, makers of the Hercules rope, Manganese and Bronze, makers of propellers, Duckham's Oil, Burrell's Colour and the East Ferry Road Engineering Works.

There were dozens of smaller firms, some short lived, some long lasting - boiler-makers and repairers, drum manufacturers, pipework engineers, pump makers, tank makers, firms making valves, tubes, tarpaulins, sacks, casks, barrels and ropes, firms making and stocking steel sections, plates, drums and doors, firms like Lenantons, established in 1837 and dealing in hardwoods and softwoods, firms specialising in lifting gear, in metal polishing and in power station repairs.

Sir Walter Besant's book, *London North of the Thames* (1911) includes the following additional industries in his list of Island producers: "saw mills; decorative earthenware works; copper-depositing works; disinfectant fluid works; antimony and gold complex ore works; van and cart works; electrical power storage company; a coal and coke company; tarpaulin manufactory; steering gear works; foundry furnisher's works".

The bigger firms supported a network of services and subsidiaries, from wharfingers and lorry drivers to the young lads collecting scrap metal on the shore for sale to the scrap metal dealers.

By 1900 the last traces of the cottages and fields which had survived the first phase of industrial development were almost gone, although at Totness Cottages, where the Ruggles family lived from 1912: "there were stables with cows and horses belonging to Mr Burgoyne who had two greeengrocer's shops in Westferry Road".

Industrial production made the Island more noisy, smelly, oily, smoky and grimy by the end of the 19th century. Limehouse-born Ben Thomas said of the early years of the 20th century:

"What a busy place it was during the week. The banging of a heavy hammer coming down on plates of metal, the drilling of holes in metal, overhead cranes lifting different metal objects, the rattling of chains, some so big they had to be lifted about by a small crane. This was going on in different factories and you could see it through the gates which were nearly always open.

One firm I remember had a small railway engine to pull railway trucks with their finished articles across the street to the warehouse. Most of the roads had big cobblestones, thick kerbstones and round-nosed gate stones. Most firms had a notice-board saying: "Public Weighbridge up to 30 Tons", outside their main gates. I have seen a low trolley with four horses pulling a heavy load of metal for the docks or engineering firms".

One of the ship-building success stories of this period was Yarrows. Alfred Fernandez Yarrow set up an engineering partnership with a Mr Hedley at Folly Wall in 1865, at the age of 23. They had four tumbledown sheds to work in and minimum capital. In the first few years, during which only 12 men were employed, the firm did little business, most of it at a loss. In 1868, almost bankrupt and with ship-building in recession, Yarrow hit on the idea of building small steam launches for use on inland lakes and rivers. This was an instant success and in the next seven years the firm built 350 steam launches.

A newspaper report of 1875 indicates that Mr Hedley left to set up his own steam launch business in Wharf Road. In the same year Yarrow, now in sole control, obtained his first government order for a steamer on Lake Nyasa.

The last quarter of the 19th century and the years leading up to the 1914-18 war saw many small-scale conflicts between nations, as governments struggled to extend their areas of influence or fend off aggressors from their territory. The warring nations and the practice of "gun-boat diplomacy" created a market for the fast and deadly torpedo boats which became a speciality of Yarrow's yard. Year by year he and his engineers improved the design of these weapons, introducing the high-tensile steel hull for lightness and strength, and the water-tube boiler for maximum fuel efficiency. Yarrow's name became known world-wide, supplying the governments of Argentina, Spain, France, Holland, Greece, Austria, Russia, Italy, Chile and Japan as well as Britain.

In 1906 Yarrow gave in to the high costs of Thames-side boat-building and moved the entire works, by rail, to Scotstoun on the Clyde. The closure of the yard was recalled by an Islander in her old age as having made her late for school one morning because: "Yarrow's whistle did not blow, Miss!" She was given two strokes of the cane on each hand for this, as the children had been warned the previous day not to wait for the hooter any more.

Mr Emms, talking about his father, said: "Dad, he came down here as a boy, he came from a place in Newcastle. He came down here as a boy, into Yarrow's shipyard...he was only a young boy and had nowhere to live. He eventually went across the road, just across there at Ferry Street on the corner there, there was a greengrocer's shop there and he used to sleep with the ponies of a night, and he was brought up by them people. (His brothers) all came down, but when Yarrow's finished there, when the shipyard finished, they went back to the place and they're all buried up there".

Ship-repair remained an important sector of the local economy for as long as the Port of London remained busy, although, like much port work, demand fluctuated with the seasons and with changes in the international trading markets. One of the great firms in this respect was Green Siley Weir (GSW) of Blackwall, where many Island men and boys were employed.

This company had its roots far back in the early days of ship-building at Blackwall. The East India company works and offices were established there in 1612, and the development of Poplar High Street, where the original East India Company chapel can still be found, dates from this time. The yard at Blackwall passed

56

through two generations of Johnsons, then to Philip Perry and later his son John. George Green was apprenticed to John Perry in 1782.

For many years the yard produced warships and merchants vessels, and by 1829 the firm had become Green, Wigrams and Green, the Perry's having given up their interest to the Wigram family, whilst George Green, who had married John Perry's daughter Sarah, was joined in due course by his son Richard. The firm was one of the largest in Europe at the time.

Fortunes changed again in 1843 when the yard was divided into two separate companies. In the 1860s, production of large ships declined dramatically as elsewhere on the Thames, and towards the end of the century Green's ceased to build even small vessels. The company amalgamated with Siley Weir & Co. in 1910. The yard was very busy in the run-up to World War One. An Islander whose parents ran a coffee shop opposite the yard entrance remembers that between 500 and 600 meals were served daily at that time. Green Siley Weir continued to operate as a ship-repair yard through two world wars,

changing its name one last time before closure in 1987, to Blackwall Engineering.

There were dry docks for ship repair all round the Island. Alf Cottage, born in 1907, whose first job was at Green Siley Weir, wrote : "There was 17 dry docks on the Island or nearby. Stewarts had three, Fletchers three, one at the back of Christ Church, Brown's, three, so you realise ship repair was a main industry".

John Stewart was born near Newcastle, at the epicentre of the Industrial Revolution. His father and grandfather were both engineers, involved in the construction of the great beam engines which can still be seen in museums in the north.

John Stewart migrated southwards after serving his apprenticeship, and worked for a number of years with a tug company in Rotherhithe. He opened the Blackwall Iron Works in Yabsley Street in 1847, and moved to a larger site at Folly Foreland on the Isle of Dogs in 1854. The company flourished for more than 50 years, building tugs and engines as well as doing ship repair, a family firm for most of that time.

The first ships in at Green's new dock, Blackwall yard, 1880; nearest the camera is the ss. *Euterpe*

"Cleopatra's Needle" the obelisk on the Thames embankment, was towed from Spain to London by a Stewart tug. Another Stewart tug sailed as far as Capetown, another even further to its new owners on South Island, New Zealand.

The firm's fortunes declined after the death of the founder, John Stewart, in 1896. His son Joseph had predeceased him and there was no one else to take over. Under new owners, who were not engineers, the company survived until the First World War when there was a brief boom in ship-repair work. It finally closed in the 1920s.

The ship repair yards gave the Island one of its classic and best-loved images - that of the ship's bowsprit stretching over the road almost into the windows of houses opposite.

These sights impressed Island boys:

"You used to get different ships at different times. Old sailormen, perhaps they'd been away a year, or perhaps eighteen months, and they'd come back for repair because in them days, all your ships had wooden bottoms like the old Cutty Sark, and they'd come in perhaps to have new timbers put in on the bottom. We used to like to see the sailormen come in, because a sailorman, a big sailorman, she'd nose her way in and then put her head - her head was right across the road, and you'd see the big figurehead on the front. As a kiddy, we used to look up, seamen used to run up and down this figurehead, when they were doing any splicing or doing the wires; we used to love watching them".

There were many firms supplying the ship-repair yards, not only iron founders, boiler makers and engineering works, but the more traditional crafts such as sail making. Lane and Neeve in the Britannia Works opposite Stewart Street were described in 1894 as: "Sail and flag makers, ships' chandlers, bunting and canvas merchants, coal, flour and all descriptions of second-hand sacks and bags, rick cloths, marquees, waterproof cloths, tarpaulins, etc".

The Isle of Dogs in this period had its share of world-class inventors and engineers. Frederick Duckham, Chief Engineer of the Millwall Dock Company, was one. Born in 1841 in Falmouth, he started work at 14 in charge of the telegraph system in the new Victoria Dock. In his spare time he studied engineering and by 1868 was appointed Clerk of Works at Millwall Dock, becoming Engineer in Chief and in 1899, General Manager. He developed new systems for handling the dock's main imports of grain and timber, making very effective use of hydraulic power. He was responsible for travelling grain bins, pneumatic grain elevators, the Eastern and Central Granaries in the Millwall Docks, the transporter which was used to convey timber across East Ferry Road into Transporter Yard (now the site of the Island Health Centre and ASDA Superstore) and many other useful devices which were brought into general use in cargo handling.

Frederick Duckham gave the Island the Mudchute. Removing silt was a continual expense for the dock companies and was a particular problem at Millwall Docks where there was an unusually large entrance. Duckham devised a dredger which had special features allowing it to operate close to the edges of the dock. A system of pressurised pipes forced the mud out of the dredger's tanks at a rate of 200 tons every 15 minutes, through an underground pipe line and into settling banks which had been constructed on dock company land on the east side of East Ferry Road. This dumping had to stop by 1900. There had been serious outbreaks of infectious diseases and the smelly mud from the dock was thought to be partly to blame. However the land settled and after being used for many years as allotments, became a community park and farm - one of Frederick Duckham's more lasting monuments.

Frederick Duckham was instrumental in founding the firm, East Ferry Road Engineering Works, which was first set up to manufacture the Duckham Weighing Machine. The company, located in East Ferry Road near *The George* hotel, became London's chief manufacturer of hydraulic machinery. Its Managing Director was Charles Parkes. His father was for many years Chairman of the Millwall Dock Company and not surprisingly the bulk of the Dock Company's orders for mechanical engineering work went to East Ferry Engineering.

All three of Frederick Duckham's sons were engineers. Frederick junior became a civil engineer and was responsible for the George V Dock; Arthur carried out experimental work in the gas industry; and Alexander founded the oil firm at Phoenix Wharf on the Isle of Dogs.

When Alexander left University at the age of 20, in 1897, petrol and diesel engines were still in the early stages of development and were posing many new challenges to the inventive skills of engineers and chemists. His awareness of this through his family and business connections, made Alexander determined to specialise in lubrication. His first job was as an analytical chemist at the Oil and Chemical Wharf owned by Flemings in West Ferry Road, where his weekly

The timber transporter built to a design by Fredrick Duckham, in Transport Yard, pictured here in 1901.

wage was fifteen shillings a week.

In 1899 he started his own business at Phoenix Wharf, Millwall, where he had a laboratory and workshop. He bought his first car. He had many friends who were motorists, including the racing driver S.F.Edge. who made a habit of visiting the Millwall works once a week to drain the sump of his engine and take on fresh oil. Alexander remained a keen motorist throughout his life, but, always interested in new developments in transport, in the 1900s he took up a fresh interest - flying. He was a founder member of the Royal Aero Club and made friends among the pioneers of the aeroplane, including Bleriot, the first man to fly across the Channel.

In 1904 his Millwall works were extended to handle the increasingly successful business. Alexander Duckham's principle was not only to produce and sell high quality oil but also to be on the look-out for new problems and their solutions. Turbine oils, ball-bearing lubricants, mould oils and soluble oils were among some of the special products of the company. Duckham was also responsible for introducing antiseptic into lubricating oil in an attempt to reduce the incidence of dermatitis amongst machine tool workers.

Whilst the motor car was slowly becoming popular and Alexander Duckham was developing lubricants for this new form of transport, hundreds of thousands of horse-shoes were needed for the horses which still provided the main pulling power on the roads. There was a horse-shoe factory on the Isle of Dogs, on the site of the present Horse Shoe Court in Ferry Street.

Here some 1,800 tons of horse-shoes were made annually in a plant employing 150 men and boys. The shoes were made from scrap iron, melted down in a furnace. The red-hot metal was pulled out in lumps which were flattened with a hammer and reheated. The hot metal was then cut into long bars, the thickness of a horse-shoe, and the bars were cut into appropriate lengths, shaped and punched.

By 1907 the firm was losing orders as private individuals began to replace their horse-drawn carriages with motor cars. A much more serious setback came when a War Office order for 100,000 pairs of horse-shoes was given to an American company. One of the directors, Albert Bayley, said: "The removal of the order from British contractors has affected us very seriously. We have had to reduce our staff by about 20 men and boys, we are working short-time and standing men off every Friday and Saturday. This means the loss of highly skilled workmen, who cannot be obtained very easily owing to the technical nature of the work".

Mr Haldane, the Minister of War, declared that in the interest of the economical administration of the Army, he could not disregard sources of supply which were satisfactory both as regards price and efficiency.

The United Horse Shoe and Nail Company went into liquidation in July 1909, one of a growing number of victims of the competition from other industrial nations which Britain was now experiencing.

The Westwoods were another family of Island industrialists. Joseph Westwood, who was born in Tipton, Staffordshire, came to live in London in 1838. He worked for Fairbairn on Millwall and became friendly with fellow-worker Robert Baillie. They worked together for some years as sub-contractors and managers for Ditchburn and Mare and they both became experienced in iron bridge construction. In 1856 they set up the firm of Westwood, Baillie, Campbell and Company at the London Yard in Manchester Road. Westwood was a Methodist and a philanthropist. His local good works included the building of a school and he was also instrumental in helping his brother-in-law John Crosby to found the Cubitt Town Methodist Church in 1862 (on the site now occupied by Crosby House). Whilst his company was building bridges in Africa, the Cubitt Town Methodists were raising funds for missionary work in the same country, including the sponsorship of one newly-baptised infant with the name "John Cubitt Town".

The firm was one of the first in the country to use wrought iron in ships, but with the collapse of the Thames ship-building industry they diverted their resources to the construction of metal bridges. In the 1880s Joseph Westwood's son founded a new firm, Joseph Westwood and Company, and took over the site in West Ferry Road previously occupied by Scott Russell and the Millwall Iron Works, opposite Cahir Street and Harbinger Road.

The international rail network was expanding and the firm took orders from Africa, South America, India and Russia. One of the contracts was the provision of a new channel span for the road bridge over the Orange River in Hopetown, Cape colony, South Africa. This bridge, originally supplied by Westwood Baillie,

had been deliberately destroyed during the Boer War. The new span, weighing 80 tons and measuring 100 feet in length, was completed within 18 days of receiving the order, allowing for the plates to be rolled in Glasgow and delivered to Millwall by rail and steamship.

Arthur Hubbard was born on the Island in 1869. His first job was as a grocer's assistant. He then went to work with his uncle at a barge-building works in Orchard Place at Blackwall. During slack times in the barge-building trade, Arthur was taken on temporarily by his father, who was foreman of the erecting department at Westwood Baillie & Co. Arthur recalled in his autobiography:

"Large contracts came from the Indian State railways. A fine bridge for over the River Indus, at a town named Sukkur, was made by this firm on the cantilever principle. The bridge opened up trade to Afghanistan in textiles, sugar, opium, saltpetre and other commodities. It was named the Sukkur Bridge and was partly built at the works".

Samuel Cutler and Sons was another Island firm renowned for engineering. Their premises were at Providence Iron Works in West Ferry Road, opposite the site later occupied by St. Edmund's Church and School. They also had a smaller site next door to the school on its southern side. Teachers in the newly-built school in the 1870s recorded in their log-books that the noise of the steel works made it difficult for the children to concentrate.

Cutlers' speciality was gas holder construction. When the Society of Engineers visited Millwall in 1879 for their annual dinner, jointly hosted by Samuel Cutler and Frederick Duckham (engineer to the Millwall Dock Company) it was reported that Cutlers "had in hand about a dozen orders for gas holders from various towns, including an immense telescope gas holder for Ipswich which is about 122 feet in diameter and is in two lifts of 32 feet depth".

The company's order book expanded to include work overseas. George Hames worked for Cutlers and wrote in his memoirs "The name of Cutler spread all over the globe - Shanghai, Hong Kong, Ismailia, Karachi, Ceylon, Jamaica, South America, Australia, South Africa and of course, Europe. Cutlers were gas work specialists, but were also builders of all kinds of tanks, oil storage, sewage farms, refrigeration plants, coal conveyors, hangars, mooring masts for the R101 and Crystal Palace aerial mast. They built the largest gas holders in the United Kingdom - Greenwich No.2 holder, originally 12,200 cubic feet but reconstructed to 8.9 million cubic feet with a steel tank 303 feet in diameter and a height of 184 feet when fully inflated, and No.1 holder with a capacity of 8.6 million cubic feet and a height of 200 feet".

Samuel Cutler was a clever engineer. He developed numerous improvements to gas holder design and was also a keen supporter of the idea of a Channel Tunnel. He wrote a book on the subject, describing the twin tunnels, single tunnels and double track which he advocated.

Cutler's employed hundreds of skilled workers - boiler-makers, riveters, platers, fitters and pattern-makers, as well as labourers and apprentices. The men of the Thompson family, who had started their working life on the Island as riveters in John Scott Russell's yard, were employed at Cutlers.

Rope-making was another important Island industry, supplying the docks and the ship-repair yards as well as markets around the world. Hempen ropes had been made in Limehouse before the Island was industrialised, and Joad and Curling's rope walk is mentioned at the beginning of the 19th century. Binks and

Bullivant manufactured wire rope on Millwall, Wrights of Millwall was well known, and the Globe Rope Works factory of Hawkins and Tipsons in East Ferry Road was celebrated for its innovative techniques and its heavy-duty hawsers.

George Hawkins was one of many nineteenth century emigrants from England to Australia. The story is that whilst cultivating his garden, he found alluvial gold, some in quite large nuggets, and enough to allow him to retire. He returned to England with his family and in 1881 invested his new fortune in a ropemaking business in partnership with his eldest son and a practical rope-maker, Mr Tipson. The business prospered and in 1910 the firm acquired a wharf and another spinning mill at Blackwall.

One of the most noticeable industrial sites on the Island - and the one with the tallest chimney to carry off the fumes - was the Lead Works in West Ferry Road. Pontifex and Wood, a varnish, colour and white lead works. was the first company on this site - hence the local name "Ponty's Chimney". A Mr. Wilcox set up a pottery on the site in 1856, a convenient neighbour, since white lead is used in glazing.

Harry and Elizabeth Oxley (nee Chamberlain), 1860s. Harry worked at the pottery in West Ferry Road. They moved to Hartlepool before 1900.

Elisabeth James, born 1865 (seated). She came to the Island with her family and worked in the pottery. In 1883 she married John Price. They had eleven children and lived in Stebondale Street, where John Price kept a Marine Store. Standing, her sister Hannah, later Harvey.

The pottery operated until 1906.

In the 1890s London's two biggest lead companies, Locke Lancaster, and W.W.& R.Johnson and Sons, amalgamated. They already had lead processing sites at Commercial Road, Burdett Road and Bridge Road Millwall. In 1895 the new company purchased the lead works in West Ferry Road opposite Greenwich Hospital. Their Commercial Road site had no water access and was given up in 1905, when part of the lead foil process was transferred to the new works at West Ferry Road. A second lead foil rolling mill was shipped to Ceylon where production costs were lower and where the company already had investment interests.

Manganese and Bronze, famous for the propellers they made for great ships such as the *Queen Mary*, followed the pottery on the site in 1906 and remained until the Second World War.

Varnish and colour making were carried out at another firm in West Ferry Road. Burrell and Company acquired part of the old *Great Eastern* site in 1888, next door to the newly-established Westwood & Co., bridge builders. In 1897 Maconochies became their neighbour on the other side.

Alfred Ewen Burrell had opened a Marine Stores in Whitechapel in 1852, specialising in marine paint. By 1870 the firm, now A.E. Burrell & Son, had several paint factories including one in Garford Street, Limehouse. Expansion continued and in the 1880s a description of their activities included:

"Contractors to British and Foreign Railways and other public works, Importers of oils, chemicals, drugs, glues, etc., Specialities: Olive Oil, Russian Glues and Lubricating Oil, Russian, Mediterranean and General Import and Export Merchants".

The take-over of what became Burrell's Wharf allowed further growth. With an expanding export trade the firm opened offices in the Canary Islands and in New South Wales.

As London's population grew, so did the demand for food. Three major food processing firms were established on the Isle of Dogs by the end of the century - Morton's, Maconochies and McDougalls. These factories, like some of packaging companies, employed many women and girls.

Food processing technology was developing in all sorts of ways during this period. The discovery of the canning process and of refrigeration, revolutionised the preservation of perishable goods such as fruit and meat. The growing urban population created huge demands for food of all kinds, and better transport and storage systems allowed large quantities to be processed and distributed to meet these new markets. All kinds of foodstuffs were brought into the docks, from the traditional West Indian sugar to frozen New Zealand meat and South American bananas. Processed, tinned and packaged goods of all kinds were exported from Britain to destinations round the world.

When he died, J.T. Morton left a quarter of a million pounds to foreign missionary work, £10 to his secretary and a thriving business to his two sons.

He started his company in Aberdeen in 1849, supplying food to sailing ships He soon realised the potential of the canning process which was then being perfected, and decided to devote his energies to the export of canned goods. He extended his Aberdeen works and also opened a new factory on Millwall in the 1870s. Later he opened a factory at Lowestoft to handle the herrings fished there, and factories were subsequently also opened in Java, India and South Africa. He had an empire within an Empire!

Bert Hiscott worked at Morton's for many years and an extract from his autobiography

A McDougall's advertising leaflet from the 19th century, with recipes on the reverse

shows how the activities of this firm, like most on the Island, were intimately bound up with the river and the docks:

"Morton's had their own fleet of barges, apart from hiring others, and the barges were named after foreign ports: *Aden, Beira, Cairo, Durban, Egypt, Fiji, Greytown, Halifax, Indore, Java, Karachi, Lahore, Malta*, etc... They also delivered by vans to the docks and of course used railway facilities to send to other ports in the UK and steamers to Bristol and Liverpool for reshipment from there. Also steamers would regularly bring goods from our Lowestoft factory to be linked up with our own goods for each customer. We also received goods from our Aberdeen factory for the same purpose".

After their father's death in 1897, Charles and Edward Morton carried on and expanded the family firm. The wide range of products included: preserved fish, meat, soup, vegetables, fruit, sausages, ham, bacon and cheese; confectionery, jams, jellies, marmalades, candied peel; pickles, sauces, potted meats and potted fish; oatmeal, barley and spices, pepper, salt, curry powders, bottled essence, tea and cocoa, bottled olives, olive oil, packaged cereals, flour and nuts; they also made custard powder and hair oils.

Morton's employed hundreds of local men and women throughout the year and many more at certain seasons, in their two factories in West Ferry Road and Manchester Road.

An equally large employer was Maconochies, whose great factory was opened in 1897 in West Ferry Road near *The Ship* public house. The famous "Pan Yan Pickle" was made here, and the firm had large contracts to supply the armed forces. The employment of dozens of women and girls from the Island and other parts of East London, and their bad working conditions, prompted the establishment of "The Welcome" Institute.

Another household name originating on the Island is McDougall's Self-Raising Flour. Alexander McDougall, the inventor of this useful domestic item, was descended from a Scottish chieftain killed at the Battle of Renfrew in 1164.

Alexander started his own working life as a humble shoe merchant in Dumfries, then moved to Manchester as a schoolmaster. His real interest was in science and mathematics and he set up his own business as a manufacturing chemist in 1845, producing his own brands of beneficial goods such as sheep dip, scouring soap and disinfectants.

When Alexander's five sons eventually joined the business, one of their concerns was to develop a patent substitute for yeast. The famous self-raising flour originated in their experiments. They set up their own mill in Manchester in 1864 and, five years later, established Wheatsheaf Mill beside the newly-opened Millwall Dock. So flour milling returned to Millwall, and, as in earlier times, it was in order to feed London's expanding

Drays and drivers in the yard at George Clark's works, Alpha Road, 1900s.

population.

For many years the five brothers between them continued to manage the three separate interests: the chemical firm, which became Cooper, McDougall and Robinson, and the two milling companies, one in the north and the other in the south.

The large Island companies cannot all be described in detail here. There were also many other companies of more modest size, often making specialist products which they supplied to the larger companies.

Most were small family businesses. Thompson and Son of Millwall was founded on Millwall in 1888 by James Thompson and his father. They made boilers, steam plant and hydraulic equipment at a works in Cuba Street, where the name was still visible on a doorway in August 2000.

James Badger Clark took Clark's Millwall Sugar Refinery to Alpha Road in 1898. Another small family business, later known as George Clark's, they supplied relatively expensive, speciality sugars to thousands of small breweries. The firm was described by descendant Peter Trafford Clark as "a prosperous, small volume, high margin type of business".

George Brockley lived at 539 Manchester Road and owned a Copper & Brass Works in Chipka Street, between the 1860s and 1904, when he died. This firm supplied copper and brass tubing and valves to local ship-repair yards.

They did contract work for John Stewart's Engineering. At the time when a works photograph was taken towards the end of the century, the firm employed at least 38 men and boys. George Brockley had no direct descendants and when he died he left his estate, valued at about £50,000, to his nephews and nieces. He left his business to his manager, James Dewar, of 49 East Ferry Road, who ran it successfully until he died in 1927.

Another man who made a small fortune while living on the Island was Joseph Cook, master smith and ship-builder. Born in Sunderland in 1844, he married Margaret Spence in 1866 and the couple moved to the Isle of Dogs in the 1870s, where Margaret had an uncle living in Barque Terrace, Manchester Road. In the 1880s Cook was living in Glengall Road and was in partnership with James Burdick in an engineering enterprise employing 60 men. They also made profitable investments in shipbuilding in the northern shipyards and when Joseph Cook died in 1934 in Blackheath he left an estate worth £250,000.

There were many of these smaller concerns, some of which had only short careers, and are remembered only as a name surviving in trade directories or on insurance maps. Who now recalls Samuel Freeth and Co., iron manufacturers, Burt, Boulton & Heywood, tar refiners, Weston & Co., cement makers, all in West Ferry Road in 1875? On the lead works site in West Ferry Road there were, at various times, as well as the companies already mentioned, an antimony works, an encaustic tile manufacturer, Vidal Fixed Analine Dyes, and the London District Telegraph Company, all gone without trace.

The small companies came and went or were absorbed into larger enterprises. Some lasted well into the 20th century, as did the giants like Westwoods and Locke Lancasters, Morton and McDougalls, Burrells and Hawkins and Tipsons, but the Great War and its aftermath was to affect them all in different ways.

9. Transport and Buildings

As more industry appeared and the population continued to grow, the Island environment became increasingly crowded, noisy and polluted due to the greater volume of road traffic rattling over the cobblestones, the expansion of the railways, the many steam ships

George Brockley and his employees at the Copper and Brass Works in Chipka Street, before 1904.

on the river and in the docks, the roar of engines, the rattle of chains, the sound of ships' sirens, the pungent aromas of spices, paint, chemicals, jam and oil, the tall chimneys belching smoke and the coal fires smouldering in two thousand homes.

Social amenities were gradually provided for the growing population. Alongside the new factories, more schools and churches were built and by the end of the century there was also better provision for sport and leisure.

The first major new transport link was the Millwall Extension Railway. The main section, opened on 18th December 1871, ran from a new station, Millwall Junction, southwards via South Dock station and three swing bridges to Millwall Dock Station (later the site of Crossharbour Station on the Docklands Light Railway). near *The George* pub. The single-track line had a 30-minute service of horse-drawn single cars.

The Millwall Dock to North Greenwich section of the line opened on 29th July 1872. A feature of the line was the 682-yard brick viaduct ending by the river near what later became Island Gardens, where North Greenwich station had a single platform, a small engine shed and a carriage siding. There was a risk of fire from steam engines and so trains were horse-drawn through the docks. In 1880 the insurance companies agreed to allow steam locomotives from Millwall Junction to North Greenwich, but horse working did not stop until 1882.

In 1874 the Great Eastern Railway bought the Blackwall-Greenwich ferry service and transferred it to a new pier at North Greenwich in order to boost traffic on the Millwall Extension Railway. This helped the Millwall Dock Company and other Island firms to draw labour more efficiently from south of the river. When the ferry was replaced by the even more efficient subway in 1902, the railway company received £8,000 in compensation for lost revenue on the ferry, though workers from south of the river still used the railway until it closed in 1926.

After 1885 the Millwall Football Club provided the railway with its heaviest traffic until the Club moved to New Cross in 1910. Their various grounds were all close to the railway in East Ferry Road behind the present Glengall Grove and in Millwall Park.

The railway was also used by Islanders for shopping trips, as Harry Anderson recalled:

"The old Islanders years ago, when they wanted to get off Millwall, they always made one form of transport favourite - that train that used to run from the foot tunnel. They used to run a passenger train, the old station was where the Poplar and

Blackwall Rowing club is now, well there was a station there...then the last stop was Harrow lane and the fare was tuppence. And it was very very handy in those days for women who were going shopping to Chrisp Street, Poplar, all they had to do was get out of the train in Harrow Lane, walk up the side street, cross East India Dock Road and they were in Chrisp Street. A very famous form of transport that was, but like everything else, they did away with it, because it was beneficial to the public and somebody wasn't making a fortune out of it".

And in fact, when the Millwall Extension Railway closed for the General Strike in 1926, and never reopened, its closure was put down to falling profits caused by the competition of the bus companies. This "very, very handy" public transport did not reappear until the Docklands Light Railway opened in 1987, once again giving easy access to Chrisp Street.

The arrival on the scene of the democratically-elected London County Council in 1889, and local borough councils ten years later, provided a much-needed impetus to public services on the Island.

One of the first jobs tackled by the new London County Council was to improve cross-river transport east of London Bridge. Work on the Blackwall Tunnel was given priority and it opened in 1897. Other river crossings were still needed between the new Tunnel and Tower Bridge. With the river so busy with shipping, and the dangers of the frequent fogs for which industrial London was notorious, ferries were simply not a reliable way of getting to work.

Arthur Hubbard recalled "a great frost" in the winter of 1895, when it was so cold that large lumps of ice floated up the Thames with each tide, and when the tide turned, went with the tide towards the estuary. The ice prevented the smaller shipping from using the river, and the ferry steam boats between the Island and Greenwich had to be withdrawn. The frost lasted several weeks and people working in Poplar had to cross from the south side by rowing boat or by one of the bridges. "Most work people were put on three-quarter time, starting at nine instead of six o'clock; the row boats did not ply during the dark hours of early morning or evening".

There were reasons better than work for going to the Isle of Dogs. Charles Croley recalled:

"To reach the East Ferry (football) ground meant for us living in Rotherhithe a journey from St.George's Steps, Deptford, to Millwall Dock Entrance by waterman's skiff. For a young lad this was indeed an adventure, for at times fog was apt to descend and I well remember on one occasion we finally landed at Wapping Old Stairs 40 minutes after departing, and on another occasion when frost and ice were present, the climbing of about 20 rungs of an ice-bound ladder up the straight side of the dock entrance needed not a small amount of courage".

The first proposal for a foot tunnel between Greenwich and the Isle of Dogs had been made in 1812, when Westferry Road was built. Nothing came of it, perhaps due to lack of investors. However, London County Council, with their wider powers and greater resources, revived the project, and Greenwich foot tunnel was opened on 4th August 1902 to replace the ferry service. The attractive circular entrances, with their glass domes, have been distinctive features of the riverside ever since.

The new tunnel, which was free, unlike the ferry service, was immediately popular and became very crowded at certain times of day. Limehouse-born Ben Thomas recalled:

"I was once going home through the Greenwich foot subway to Millwall, not knowing it was so late, when I came against the rush of home-going workmen. I never thought I would get through the crowd, it was so dense with dockers and workmen from different factories".

Bert Hiscott thought that carrying a bike up and down the tunnel stairs (before the lifts were installed) was not an improvement, especially when a girl friend's cycle had to be carried too. John Pearson wrote: "it did not seem nearly such fun to journey to Greenwich by subway. The ferry boat thrilled but the subway was rather awe-inspiring at first. Until one got used to it there was rather a sense of being "shut in" in negotiating this five to ten minute walk under the Thames".

Workers coming from the north of the Island faced a different problem. The lock bridges in Westferry Road and Prestons Road were only wide enough for a single lane of vehicles. They were both a hazard and an inconvenience. In 1879 Poplar District Board asked the London County Council to install new bridges, having failed to persuade the dock companies to carry out improvements. Amongst the complaints they considered the following was minuted:

"Read letter from Mr James Dewar of 100 East Ferry Road dated 20th inst. and calling attention to the dangerous and disgraceful state of the West India Dock Bridges at Blackwall. Surely it was time some better and safer bridges were provided. On the 18th instant in the evening his wife had a severe fall through slipping off the narrow path on

Port of London Authority railway engine and staff, about 1910.

the South Dock bridge, bruising and shaking herself very much besides spoiling her dress. The bridges were positively dangerous the traffic had much increased and whoever is responsible he presumed that it was the Board's duty to see that the public highways were safe and in good order".

This is the same James Dewar who worked for George Brockley and who was to inherit the company in 1904.

In the 1890s new and wider bridges, operated by hydraulic machinery, were installed at all but the Kingsbridge entrance to the Millwall Docks. This did not satisfy local demand and in 1902 there was a series of meeting attended by local politicians and employers, at which attention was drawn to:

"...the present extremely unsatisfactory facilities for pedestrians and vehicular traffic to and from the Isle of Dogs, which is the immediate cause of much inconvenience to manufacturers and others.. and the source of frequent delays and sometimes dangers to the residents Mr Willett, a cartage contractor, said that the dock companies had practically closed the Island to and from Poplar and claimed that: "It frequently happened that a man and horse had to lose a whole day in one journey to Poplar".

Ben Thomas's recollection from the early 20th century illustrates the bottlenecks at the bridges:

"When the 1914-18 war was on it was ever so noisy and busy when I have gone over to Millwall from Limehouse, when work was over hundreds of men and boys would be coming along the Westferry road to Limehouse way. The clump, clump of their heavy boots, for they nearly all wore hobnail boots; horses and carts trudging along the uneven cobble-stoned road; the noise of men and boys talking and joking to one another.

Sometimes a road bridge would be opened to let a boat in or out of the docks, when you would see one block of men waiting for the bridge to close, when it closed there would be one big rush of people to make up for time, while waiting. The same scene of home-going workmen would be going towards Poplar".

The idle passer-by might watch the crowds or wave to the sailors on ships passing through the lock. Another notable sight was the diver: "Often as you would go over the bridge you would see those old-type divers' platforms with the diver sitting on, having his helmet screwed on. Inspecting the lock gates and things like that. He used to sit there with these great big heavy boots they used to wear and then he had his helmet screwed on with the little bars over the front..".

One hindrance to traffic which was abolished was the toll on both access roads onto the Island. That went in 1885 when both Westferry Road and East Ferry Road were adopted by the local authorities. A less popular move by Island businessmen and ratepayers was the abolition of the right of way along the river wall, or Marsh Wall, in 1875. This was the subject of an exchange of angry letters in the local press, but business interests won the day and what remained of the old pathway was closed.

The factories, wharves and warehouses on the Island, as well as the docks themselves, created a constant demand for the transport of goods. Many firms had their own fleet of carts and lorries, but not all, and a number of Island companies prospered, from small beginnings, by providing a haulage service. Davison's Garage was one.

George Middleditch, from Hollesby in Suffolk, arrived in Mellish Street with his family in 1891. He purchased a local horse-bus company from John Hames and started to operate from Cheval Street. John Hames set up another bus service for Cubitt Town, running from the *Princess of Wales* in Manchester Road to the Iron Bridge in Canning Town.

Middleditch's bus ran from the Millwall Dock Tavern, also known as the *Dock House* (outside the present Westferry Printers), to West India Dock Station. It held 10 people inside and four on top with the driver. There was a small trap-door in the roof. The driver would put a hand through this and one passenger, having collected the penny fares, would puts them in his hand. The journey is described in *Off the Track in London (1900)* : "Just outside the West India dock station there is a little one-horse bus which takes you by a winding way of high black walls, broken here and there by bridges and wharves and the towering masts of ships, to Millwall".

In Harry Anderson's recollection, this was an alternative way of getting to Chrisp Street:

"...when I was a kid, they used to have horse buses on this Island, used to run from Millwall Docks to near Charlie Brown's famous pub, there's a railway bridge there and that's as far as the bus went, well, when I was a kid, my mother used to give me a shopping bag and a list for the groceries she wanted, used to give me the money and a penny to ride on top of the bus, we., I could either ride on the bus with an empty shopping bag, and then walk to Chrisp Street, or I could walk up to Chrisp Street and come back with a loaded shopping bag and get the bus and ride home. My mother only gave me a penny fare one way... I mean, things were very bleak in those days, you know, very bleak..".

Most people walked, according to Mrs Lowery, born in 1890: "Yes, we walked this Island. There was no transport or anything - there used to be an old bus...and then, this side, they had the train there, up to Poplar. But the majority of people on the Island have walked - walked this

Divers employed by the Millwall Dock Company, about 1900. Seated second from left is Edward Humphrey, born 1859. He worked for the Company all his life and lived in Pier Head Cottages, West Ferry Road.

Island years and years ago. But I should think doing so much walking hasn't hurt me".

By 1902 George Middleditch had moved into 227 West Ferry Road, where buildings with stabling for 16 horses, a hay-loft over an engine-driven chaff cutter, sick bay, wheelwright's shop, paint shop, covered washing area and open yard, together with a family house and four flats, had all been constructed by local builders Fred and T.R. Thorn.

Meanwhile James Davison of Millwall, who had been serving in the Boer War as a farrier's assistant, came home and set himself up as a farrier in a yard adjacent to Middleditch. In 1907 he married the girl next door, George Middleditch's daughter, Anne.

George Middleditch handed on his business to his son Albert in 1910, but after three years Albert decided to sell up because of competition from a motor bus service which had just started.

James Davison acquired the lease on Middleditch's premises, sub-let some of the stables and expanded his business. As a farrier, his work included shoeing the magnificent horses of the police and fire brigades. When the First World War broke out, he began to provide a haulage transport service, one of his many local customers being Fletcher Son and Fearnall, ship repairers in West Ferry Road. He also became a Special Constable. He is remembered as the blacksmith for small boys: "His forge was behind the coffee shop next to the Dock House, us boys had iron hoops, when they broke we took them to Mr Davison who welded them in the fire and charged a ha-penny".

Herbert Brothers was another local transport firm. They had 20 horses stabled in West Ferry Road and undertook work for the United Shipping Company. The family lived in Island Gardens in a house facing Greenwich Park.

Horse-drawn transport has vanished so completely by the 21st century that it is easy to forget how the presence of the horse once dominated the streets, and created an entire industry and sub-culture of farriers, blacksmiths, saddle-makers, coachmen, carters, hay and corn dealers, wheelwrights and waggoners, all with their specialised knowledge of handling horses.

These characters fascinated Island children before the First World War.

"At the bottom of our back yard was a firm of carters, Middleditch and Quy by name. Two men, one short, one tall, who wore tweed jackets with leather elbow patches and leather gaiters over what looked like jodhpurs. The horses used in their trade were stabled in the yard adjoining ours

Horse-drawn bus leaving West India Dock Station, 1900s. Seated in front on top is Eleanor Thurgood (later Lapwood) born 1892.

The crew of the Island horse-bus, run by George Middleditch. Hackney drivers in the back row, Albert Middleditch on the left and Robert Dodkin second from right. Bus drivers in the middle row, with Bill Digby second from right. Stable boys in front. Standing on the left is William Davison, the farrier

and they frightened me as a child as they kicked in their stalls.

In Cheval Street, the other side of Janet Street, was the blacksmiths where Mr Lathan would be hard at work at his anvil, clad in long leather apron. We saw him as we passed by on our way to St.Luke's School.... the boys used to sauce him and he would throw buckets of water over them. But us girls used to love to watch him shoe the horses. My mother bought one of the horse buses and when she moved to Laindon; she used to stay in it while my father built us a small bungalow there".

There was another blacksmith's shop belonging to the Griffin family under the arches of the Millwall Extension Railway in Douglas Place (the site of the present Island Gardens Station). As well as shoeing horses, blacksmiths did all kinds of metal work, repairs and minor engineering jobs.

Horse droppings sustained millions of flies which were a significant health hazard in shops and homes. They also provided a larder for the thousands of sparrows who chirruped and

fluttered on the streets. Horses were less easily controlled than the motor car and potentially just as dangerous. Children were sometimes injured or killed by horse-drawn vehicles. Rider-less horses had a complete disregard for traffic rules. Mr Clarke, a messenger for the dock company, recalled:

"In 1881 a mounted messenger service, to ships, etc., was instituted to convey bills and letters from the town office of the dock company next to Fenchurch Street Railway Station. It was maintained by three horses and three boy riders, one mount and messenger being held in reserve in case of accidents. On one occasion my horse fell down in Garford Street. I was left in the road, and the horse dashed over the bridge and was stopped at the old toll gate outside Mortons".

Poorly lit roads with open drainage ditches were another hazard Although West Ferry and Manchester Roads were provided with gas street lamps, East Ferry Road lagged behind. It was claimed in a letter to the East End News in 1890 that "the road has been very little used after dark, simply for want of lamps. It is only recently that fences have been put to to guard against anyone falling into the ditches on dark and foggy night (an event of common occurrence)". Bert Hiscott, a young lad at the turn of the century, said of East Ferry Road: "...it was a rendezvous for courting couples and it was not considered nice to be found there after dark. But small boys would ride down on bikes and shine their lamps on the lovers who did not appreciate that one bit".

Research into the architecture of industrial buildings on the Island has shown that it was often makeshift.. The decline of shipbuilding in the 1860s and the varied fortunes of ship-repair yards after that, resulted in dilapidation and lack of investment in new buildings on some riverside sites. Instead, old buildings were hastily adapted for new purposes, then altered again as use changed or businesses contracted and expanded. Records of premises at Stewarts Dry Dock in Manchester Road (where Thomas Pitcher had had his works early in the century) illustrate both the muddle of the yard and its long-term deterioration.

In 1889 the dry docks was described in a sales brochure as having: "Concrete and wooden bottoms, wood sides and wood stages. A smith's shop, engine and boiler house, chimney shaft, machine and saw sheds, stores, general stores, saw pits with joiners' shop over, large mast house and shop with sail loft over, range of offices on two floors with gatekeepers office and a foreman's dwelling".

The fixed plant consisted of: "24 horse-power beam engine with two 18-inch pumps, boiler, fan, saw bench, punching and shearing machine, smith's forge, bellows, plate and angle iron furnace, levelling slats, steam kiln, direct acting pumps and boiler, cranes, capstones, winches, shafting vices and benches".

Stewart's dry dock was the one from which ships' bowsprits were often seen protruding in that classic image of the Island. In 1912 the yard, parts of which were by then over 100 years old, was assessed for taxation and was described as follows:

"Comprises two dry docks 230 and 265 feet long respectively, ground floor store with corrugated iron roof, very poor condition, old timber joiners' shop, second floor office and store under, brick built very poor order, small building raised on stanchions open underneath, very old, bad repair' brick and slate sheds old and dilapidated, small brick slate sheds".

The picture was mixed however. Some firms, like ship-repair yards, were deteriorating. Others, representing new inventions and pioneering development, were expanding and building. Morton's and Maconochies each erected imposing new factories on their respective sites in the 1880s and 1890s. Duckhams and Hawkins and Tipsons each extended their premises in this period.

Inflammable materials, the naked flames of candles, gas lights and oil lamps and inadequate safety precautions led to frequent fires followed by rebuilding. McDougall's original Wheatsheaf Mills were completely destroyed in a blazing inferno in the 1890s and had to be rebuilt. At Hawkins and Tipson's the Millwall Extension Railway crossed the yard on a brick viaduct and sparks from the engine often started small fires amongst the bales of hemp. On one occasion the original mill was burnt down when a man carrying out repairs left a blow lamp burning unattended. The wooden upper floor, being soaked in machine oil, was soon alight and all the spinning machines dropped through the floor onto the drawing frames below.

In 1904 a new Fire Station - still with horse-drawn engines - was built in West Ferry Road opposite the lead works.

Next door to the rope walk was the Mudchute, the earth and clinker bank enclosing acres of deep mud. One morning after heavy rain this 25-foot high bank was observed to be moving slowly forward, crushing the buildings in its path. The Dock Company officials were summoned and immediately set about installing a wall of piles at the foot of the bank. Disaster was averted but the Chief Engineer, Frederick Duckham, was reported to have said that the whole factory, and many of the people in it, might have been swept away without prompt action.

The large population of hard-working people, many of them of a tough and independent cast of mind and unused to the constraints of law and order, together with the vast amount of valuable goods in transit, brought the attention of the authorities to the need to protect private property and exercise some restraints on public behaviour.

The Metropolitan Police had been in existence since 1828, but responsibility for policing the Island had remained with Poplar watch-house until a police station opened in East India Dock Road in 1859. The Island's first police station opened in Manchester Road in 1865 (on the site of the present George Green's School). There was room for eight sergeants and twelve police constables in the living quarters and for a number of prisoners in three cells. When a police station was opened in West India Dock Road in 1879, the first Limehouse Police Station, it took over responsibility for the west or Millwall side of the Island. In the 1860s the river police station in Coldharbour had been transferred to a ship, *Scorpion*, moored at Folly Wall. The ship was replaced with a new land-based station in Coldharbour in 1895. Other police presence on the Island included the Great Eastern Railway Police and the Millwall Dock Police. The latter was combined with the London and India Dock Police in 1909 to form part of the Port of London Authority Police.

Education and religion are gentler ways of bringing an unruly population into line and in the second half of the 19th century the Island was provided with its share of schools and churches. In the 1870s, day schools held in church buildings, and a handful of private schools, made up the Island's education provision. Arthur Hubbard, the son of an engineer, went to a private school run by a Mr Westwood, who he described as "a stately old gentleman and a wonderful disciplinarian, for he liked well-behaved boys and if they did not behave he would know the reason why. The fee was fourpence a week. There was no playground, therefore no playtime. The other private schools were kept by mistress, Mrs Coulson and Miss Baldwin, both catered for girls, the latter mistress taught piano and music lessons".

The Education Act of 1870 created the London School Boards with powers to finance the provision of school places for every child. Within 10 years, all the Island's principal schools had been built, though most had to be enlarged within the following 20 years. At the same time there was a spate of new church building.

To cater for children in the expanding Cubitt Town, Glengall Road Board School was built on the corner of Glengall Road and Manchester Road in 1875. Arthur Hubbard recalled that the school was built on pasture land where he had seen sheep grazing. When he started there on the first day it was opened: "everything was clean and new, the desks, books, slates, pencils and maps hanging on the walls, all had a newness, even the asphalted playground covered with shells was a pleasure to walk on".

St.Luke's church on the corner of Strafford Street and Church Road,(later Alpha Road) was opened in 1870, replacing the original "Iron church" which was also a school. This building was too small to hold the children who wanted to attend and St.Luke's Church of England School was opened in West Ferry Road in 1873, financed by both public and private funds. A fund to extend the school was opened in the 1890s.

The small school attached to Christ Church, in Billson Street, was sold to the London School Board in 1876, to become Cubitt Town School. It was replaced by a much larger building in Saunders Ness Road in 1891. (The original school became the church hall).

The new St. Edmund's church replaced St.Edwards in 1876, when the consecration was performed by Cardinal Manning. In his speech he recalled the old church as having had a leaking roof, unglazed windows and cracked walls, and he praised the magnificent new building with its walls decorated with religious murals.

St. Edmund's School in West Ferry Road was built next to the new church in the 1870s. The premises were later rebuilt on a much larger scale by the local authorities.

A new London Board School, Harbinger School, replaced the old British Street School in 1908.

All these new schools of this period were built in similar style, tall brick buildings with large windows surrounded by a hard-surface playground. They all had much the same layout as Glengall Road Board School, described by Arthur Hubbard as: "...a three-storied building. The infants department was on the ground floor, the girls department on the middle floor, the boys on the top floor".

Under a London County Council initiative to provide free secondary schooling for bright children, Millwall Central School was opened in 1906 in the Westferry end of Glengall Road. A small school in Janet Street provided teaching for children with special needs.

By the end of the century, every child had a free school place, but long before that, in the 1850s, an Act of Parliament had allowed local councils to provide libraries and books out of the rates. Poplar had more urgent issues to tackle, and it was not until 1894 that a public library was opened in Poplar High Street. Donations from local businessmen reduced the charge on the rates. A year later the Isle of Dogs got its branch library in Island Gardens, at Osborne House, a converted villa which had previously been home to local businessmen. In 1905, thanks to a grant of £15,000 from Andrew Carnegie, the Cubitt Town Library was opened in Strattondale Street. It had a reading room and public hall

The London City Mission began holding

services in a tent in Glengall Road, near the new school, in the 1870s. Such large numbers attended that they were eventually able to build a permanent Mission Hall on the site.

The growth of the Island population merited its division into a third Anglican parish and a third church, first named St.Paul's, was established in a wooden hut which had been used by the Millwall Dock contractors. Money was raised for a permanent building and the new church, now named St John's to avoid confusion with the existing Presbyterian church of St.Paul's, was consecrated in December 1872.

St.John's Church of England School had already been built close by in 1869. It consisted of a single-storey mixed classroom and a smaller room for infants. This building was enlarged at the turn of the century.

Around each new Anglican church were other buildings, principally the church hall and vicarage. The vicarages of Christchurch and of

Artist's impression of the new Cubitt Town Methodist Chapel, 1905.

St.Luke's still survive and have much the same accommodation as that provided for the Victorian vicar of St.John's : "...night nursery, day nursery, bathroom with cold water supply and fireplace, large bedroom, spare bedroom, servants' bedroom, W.C., landing and stairs, dining room, drawing room, study, entrance hall, W.C., entrance lobby, small room, kitchen, pantry, scullery and coal place. There were bells to summon the servants and the St. John's vicarage stood in a walled garden between Castalia Street, East Ferry Road and Galbraith Street.

St. John's Church buildings were extended by the end of the century, again under pressure from the growing population. A mission hall was added in the 1880s and a two-storey workmen's club in the 1890s. In 1900 a second clubhouse was built for boys.

The Methodists too were expanding. There

was a Wesleyan chapel in Stebondale Street and on Millwall the Alpha Road chapel was opened in 1887, replacing a small chapel in Cheval Street. In Cubitt Town, the Primitive methodists also needed more space and they raised the money to enlarge their premises in Manchester Road, opening the new chapel in 1905

The new schools, churches and chapels and the public library added an imposing new element to the Island's built environment. They also brought together adults and children from diverse backgrounds to learn common beliefs and skills, contributing to the creation of a community with shared experiences and ideals.

As the Island's population grew progressively poorer towards the end of the century, it received progressively more attention from well-meaning members of the middle class, who felt a calling to work in "the slums of the East End".

In 1896 Brother Aelred Carlyle attempted to re-found the Benedictine way of life within the Anglican church, choosing the Isle of Dogs as his testing ground. He gathered round him a group of like-minded young men and they acquired a house in Glengall Road. They surrounded their small monastery with a high wooden fence and painted the words "the Priory" over the door. These monks moved off to more spacious premises before the First World War.

Nonconformist missions multiplied by the end of the century. A Sunday School Demonstration in the 1890s included processions from each of the following: Salvation Army Mission Hall; Sailors' Institute Millwall Dock; Presbyterian Church West Ferry Road; Primitive Methodist Chapel West Ferry Road; Wesleyan chapel and London City Mission, Stebondale Street; the Tobago Street Mission and the Assembly Hall Mission, Glengall Road.

St.Cuthbert's Church was a Mission church and was by way of being a "poor relation" of Christchurch. It was begun in 1897 by the Reverend Richard Free and Mrs Free, who first held services in an upstairs room, then in a stable, then moved into the new St.Mildred's Settlement, whilst funds were raised for the new church.

St.Cuthbert's stood on the corner of Cahir Street and West Ferry Road and was set amidst some of the oldest and poorest housing on the Island - run-down cottages in side-turnings and dilapidated terraces along the main road. It was a modest building, with a main hall on the ground floor and the church itself upstairs. The vicar and his wife lived in a house nearby.

St.Mildred's Settlement was also opened in

St. Cuthbert's church on the corner of Cahir Street.

1897. This institution was aimed at women and girls in particular. The dedicated middle-class women who came there to work hoped to bring new standards of child-care, cleanliness and domestic economy to those they saw as being in need of instruction in these matters. St.Mildred's was in West Ferry Road, near to St.Paul's Presbyterian Church.

At the same time a canteen for women and girls, The Welcome Institute, was opened in temporary accommodation. Its founder, Mrs Price, a wealthy widow, had been moved by the sight of the women and girls who worked at Maconochie's sitting outside on the kerbstones to eat their mid-day meal, and she determined to provide them with shelter. Her work proved popular and she was able to obtain land from Lady Margaret Charteris (grand-daughter of William Mellish) and money from her rich friends for a purpose-built hall with living accommodation. The plain-fronted building, which later became the Dockland Settlement No.2, was opened in 1905 in East Ferry Road, near the Millwall Extension Railway viaduct.

Now that working men had the vote, meeting places for political groups were needed. The pubs were already used for gatherings of all kinds - trade unions, friendly societies, sports clubs and groups like the ancient Order of Foresters and the "Buffs". The Conservatives and Unionists had a hall in Glengall Road. The Liberal Party met next door to the Primitive Methodist Chapel in Manchester Road. In 1897 the Isle of Dogs Progressive Club, forerunner of Poplar Labour Party, opened its own purpose-built premises in Pier Street, with rooms for meetings, reading and entertainment.

Outdoor sport and recreation became more organised during the 1890s, as a result of both private and public initiative.

Public baths were provided by the local authority in Glengall Road (later Tiller Road) and East India Dock Road. In 1895, Island Gardens was opened, with its flower-beds, bandstand, children's play area and magnificent views over the river to Greenwich. The North Greenwich Bowls club, whose members were principally rate-paying shop-keepers, had their ground in Island Gardens. Mr Hames set up the Ivanhoe Sports Ground (also called Athletics Ground, and Cricket Ground) in West Ferry Road during the 1890s.

Football was played on various official and unofficial sites around the Island. Millwall Football club, the Island's professional team, had grounds in two successive places in East Ferry Road, one on fields behind the Lord Nelson, where cricket had also traditionally been played.

There was some new house-building during this period. The bulk of the Island's housing stock had been built in mid-century and had never been high quality. It continued to deteriorate slowly, neglected by both landlords and tenants who lacked either the will or the means, or both, to carry out improvements. The work of the Medical Officer of Health and the Poplar Board of Works remained a constant battle against blocked drains and crumbling brickwork.

Flooding at high tide, with storm waters filling the drains and causing sewage to back up, remained a problem in spite of new equipment to limit the damage.

The Minutes of the Metropolitan Board of Works record floods on the Island in the 1860s and in the 1880s.

J.W Bazalgette, Engineer to the MBW, described conditions on 30th July, 1888, as follows:

"The rain commenced at 3pm. At 5.15pm the water had risen to flooding level and continued to rise to four feet six inches above that level. At 10 pm the tidal flaps and perstocks were opened to their full extent, being four hours after high water - the water having fallen in the meantime in the sewers - the tide and water were falling rapidly. The flooding was mostly at high tide, the rain being spoken of as "absolutely tropical" and such as had not been witnessed before on the Island, completely mastering the two temporary centrifugal systems....Many of the inhabitants went to the engine shed during the time and saw that everything was being done by the men and the engines that could be done, but such a deluge occurring at high water could not be mastered by the two engines and pumps".

In 1867 a serious outbreak of cholera swept

through the East End, supposedly originating in Poplar and adding greatly to the misery of the starving unemployed. As always, the authorities expressed concern, but they had limited powers to change anything. An outbreak of scarlet fever in Cubitt Town in the winter of 1879-80 was blamed partly on infected children mingling with others in the new schools. Some of the houses in Cubitt Town were reported at this time to be in: "a deplorable insanitary condition; many had their kitchens flooded from time to time with rain water and sewage, rendering the basements damp and foul, others were damp from bad material.... Leaking roofs and spouts were common, as were defective traps and sinks, drains and closets...Cisterns were found without covers in dirty back kitchens, others literally inside water closets and supplying both houses and closets".

The uncovered ditch which drained the Mudchute was reported to be "a general receptacle for dead animals and vegetable garbage," and in 1895 the mud-shoot was still being used as a tip for the contents of a cess-pit privy inside the docks. At the turn of the century the authorities managed to enforce its closure as a dumping ground and the land was left to harden off. Old Islanders recalling their boyhood said it wobbled "like a jelly" when they sneaked past the PLA policeman to play in this forbidden territory.

In 1897, 130 cases of diphtheria were reported in Cubitt Town, an alarming increase on the 51 cases reported the previous year. Infections were thought to spread through parents sending children to school with what they thought was only an ordinary cold, and also through the sharing of slates and pencils. Typhoid and measles were other killers and many families suffered the loss of children and teenagers.

In the 1880s, old sailing warships moored in the Thames at Long Reach were used as isolation hospitals for adults and children infected with disease. People from the East End were taken in horse-drawn ambulances to North Pier in Coldharbour and then transported in special small steamers to the hospital ships. For many people, this was their last journey. The steamers were built by Island companies and were similar to river steamers, except that their funnels were painted yellow.

A hospital, the Joyce Green, replaced the ships early in the century. The practice of isolating infected patients continued for many years, until eventually inoculation programmes eliminated the deadly diseases. Other illnesses were treated at home or in Poplar Hospital which now treated women and children as well as the working men for whom it had been established.

Increasing awareness of the connection between infectious diseases and poor housing led the middle class to move into more exclusive residential districts by the end of the 19th century

Thomas Cole's research into the social structure of the Island population showed that in general large employers had moved out of their Island villas and onto the heights of Blackheath or similar suburbs by the end of the century. The large houses on factory sites which had been their homes became offices, or were used by foremen and managers unless they were demolished to make room for new workshops.

In spite of this general trend, there were still enough business people living on the Island to merit a cautious amount of speculative building at the end of the century.

Canal Row, the cottages which Thomas Pitcher had built for his workmen near the entrance to the South West India Dock, was demolished in 1880. Local auctioneer and surveyor Bradshaw Brown, who lived on Blackheath, proposed to the then owners, the Dock Company, that he should find builders and tenants for 20 substantial houses on the site.

Bradshaw Brown's project never came off, the price asked for the land being too high. Instead the Dock Company sold the land to William Warren, an estate agent in East India Dock Road. In the 1890s a terrace of three and four-storied houses, with bay windows and basements, was built on the site.

Warren's deal with the Dock Company was negotiated by Harry Hooper, estate agent of 173 West Ferry Road, a business address he shared with Bradshaw Brown. Warren and Hooper were also directors of the Orient Permanent Building Society, who financed the purchase of some of the new houses at a price of £390 each.

These houses were designed for families with servants to live in a certain amount of comfort and cleanliness. They had inside toilets and running water, back gardens, good-sized rooms and a view of the river - privileges shared by few other Islanders at that time. Glen Terrace, as the new houses were called, was occupied and owned by professional or business men and their families. There were not enough Island families who could afford a whole house in Glen Terrace, however, and nine of the 20 houses were in two-family occupation by the end of the 1890s.

There was only one other comparable development on the Island in this period and that was Charteris Terrace, in East Ferry Road behind Millwall Fire Station, built in the 1900s. Professional people like schoolteachers were among the residents.

In the 1880s land to the north of Cubitt Town was developed for housing by local builders and small-scale investors. The northern end of East Ferry Road, as well as Plevna, Galbraith, Launch, Castalia, Roserton and Chipka Streets were all built up in streets of two-storeyed terraced houses, which were quickly occupied.

Although there was vacant land on the Millwall side of the Island, there was no new house building, even though it was desperately needed by the end of the century. Hundreds of people walked to work in Millwall and Cubitt Town from their homes in adjacent neighbourhoods, because there was no available housing close by.

The Reverend Richard Free was one of the great champions of the working people of the Island. In an article in *The Builder* in August 1901, he vividly and sympathetically described the homeward bound workers, some of whom: "...walk an hour or more to and from work". He went on to say that house building for workers was prevented: "...by the high price of land, between £1,250 per acre leasehold to £6,000 per acre freehold, and by the high rates, the highest in London", and that existing houses and rows of old cottages were demolished, their inhabitants evicted without the prospect of new accommodation and new factories built on the site for yet more workers. He may have been referring to Maconochie's giant food processing plant, opened in 1897, the year he arrived on the Island, and where there had previously been cottages.

Though employers and business people and some families of skilled workers occupied a whole house, multiple occupancy was commonplace among both skilled workers and the poorer sections of Island society. For the majority, the need to keep costs down by living close to work and sharing the rent remained important considerations. Overcrowding increased as newcomers continued to arrive and the population reached its peak of around 21,000 by 1900.

10. Island people

The growth of the Island population to over 21,000 men, women and children within this period was due to both natural increase and to continued migration from other parts of the British Isles.

Some of the families who had arrived in the prosperous period of ship-building had by now settled down and raised another generation of Islanders.

David Thompson, who was six when his family arrived from Scotland in the 1850s, was a 30-year-old married man by 1881, described as a boiler maker, living at 136 West Ferry Road. His wife Sophie, a Millwall woman, was 22. They had two children, Sophia, aged 1 year and William, 10 days old.

The first Martini had arrived on the Island, aged 18, on the day Lord Nelson was buried. He found work in the docks, married a local girl and settled in Manilla Street. They had four children who also settled down on Millwall. Their eldest son also had four children and his eldest son was Charles Martini, who lived on Millwall all his 97 years and worked for the wire rope manufacturers, in Strafford Street, for 60 of them.

Arthur Hubbard, who was born in 1869, recorded that his maternal grandfather, a Mr Norman, had come from Newmarket to work in the iron ship-building trade. His daughter married Arthur's father, foreman engineer at Westwoods, and they had a family of nine boys and four girls. Four boys died in infancy, the rest grew to adulthood on the Island.

There were many more of these growing families and their numbers were constantly increasing with the arrival of others from all parts of the British Isles, attracted by the great variety of work available on the Island for men and women,

Top left: Alice and Joe Bulloch, of West Ferry Road. Jo is thought to have been a stevedore. Joe's great-grandaughter, Joan Jordan, remembered him in old age, waxing the ends of his moustache and twisting his kiss-curls into shape. "How he loved his pint of porter, he'd plunge the hot poker into it and it would fizz everywhere".
Top right: Mr and Mrs Mair, friends or relatives of the Hiscott family.
Bottom left: Catherine Cane, born in Ireland in 1872 and her husband Alfred. They lived in Manilla Street. Catherine, when young, used to sell fresh fish from a barrel at the dock gates. Alfred worked at Bullivant's rope works. They had "about" 14 children, of whom eight survived.
Bottom right: Catherine Mary Anne Studd (nee Elis) and her husband George. Catherine was born in Ramsey, Essex. She became a domestic servant in Kirby-le-Soken and met George when he was quartermaster on the Cutty Sark. As the ship often came into the Millwall Docks, they settled on the Island in Cahir Street. In later life, George went into partnership with Mr Maltby in a stevedoring firm in East Ferry Road.

Probably a Miss Mustin, and definitely the first wife of David Thomas, engineer from Glamorganshire. The couple met on board ship as emigrants to Australia. They married and had two children and she died whilst still young.

The widower David Thomas returned to the UK and settled on the Isle of Dogs, where he re-married and had a further eight children. One of the children from his first marriage was Ernest Thomas, father of Daisy, later Daisy Clayden

young and old, skilled or unskilled.

George Spruson was the son of a "Labourer in coals" who had migrated from Essex to London in the first half of the century. George became a white metal worker in ship-building and married Elizabeth Pomroy of Stewart Terrace, Cubitt Town. Her father was a dock labourer and her grandfather had been an under-gardener at Wilton House before also becoming a dock labourer. George and Elizabeth lived in East Ferry Road where their first son James was born in 1899.

Edward Saulter was a coachsmith and he married Caroline Baxter in Bethnal Green in 1863. Their eight children were born in Islington but by 1891 they were all living on the Isle of Dogs where Edward and three of his sons were labourers in an iron works and Frederick, the

eldest, was a riveter in a gas holder yard, probably Cutler's. Descendants of this family lived on the Island until the Second World War.

The origins of many families whose descendants still lived on the Island in the late 20th century, can be traced back to the second half of the 19th century.

Mr Bensley, born in 1900, said that his father and grandfather walked to Millwall from Long Melford in Suffolk, when his dad was 12 or 13 years old. "My old grandfather got a job at John Bellamy's".

In 1881 Thomas Clayden was living at 1, Mast House Cottages He had been born in Bailey in Essex. His wife Margaret was Irish. They had six children, aged 13, 11, 9, 7, 5 and 4 months, all born locally. One of Thomas's grandson's grew up to marry Daisy Thomas of Cubitt Town. Daisy died in 1998, having lived on the Island all her 96 years.

William Pye was another Essex man. He moved to the Island as a boy to work in the new Millwall Docks. In 1881 he and his wife Jenny, from Limehouse, were living at 2, Devonshire Terrace. William and his male descendants for three generations remained on the Island and became stevedores, the last one, George Pye, only retiring from this work when the docks finally closed in the 1970s.

Stories of how people got here give a sense of determination and strength of character. Now and again more of the personality of one of these Victorian Islanders comes to light, either in a photograph or as a distant memory.

Bert Hiscott's grandfather Ward grazed cows on the Island and had a cab business ferrying ships' captains to the City and West End and back again. He also had a milk round: "I remember my grandfather as a bull of a man with a huge beard and as a mattter of course he used to have a tot at each pub he served with milk and did two rounds a day. He had ten children, of which my mother

Top left: Thomas Bean, general labourer, of East Ferry Road.
Top right: Isabella Maria Lunn, born 1875, mother of eight children.
Bottom left: Edith Ellen Wilson, born 1884, died 1928. Her father, a seamen, died young, her mother was a midwife. Edith went to St. John's School, worked at the pram and mangle company and married Harry Horner They lived in Galbraith Street near her mother, and had three boys and two girls. She took in washing to earn extra money.
Bottom right: John Hubbard, born in Janet Street, Millwall, about 1840. His father, William Hubbard, was a cement burner. John became a wire rope maker, married Mary Broderick in 1862 and they lived in Tooke Street.

79

The so-called "Greek Gypsies" on Millwall.

was the eldest. After his wife died he eventually at the age of 60-odd years ran away with another man's wife and lived in the countryside until he was about 80".

Mr Morton, according to his obituary in the *Westminster Gazette*, was dour and uncommunicative. He never spoke of his home and family, had no sentiment, no appreciation of beauty. He was a rigid Sabbatarian - no Sunday opening for him - strictly honest, exact and just, as he understood justice. He read the Times and daily reports of his business, his Bible and books of religion. He augmented his canning fortune by buying up a large area of land in Theydon Forest, having all the trees cut down and plain, square houses built on it.

Kit Bradley's father came from Ireland on the way to America, but meeting his future wife, who had no intention of going to America, he settled in London: "...my father stayed on at school until he was eighteen. He was a very clever man. He came over with the intention of going to America. His uncle had a carpet factory there and he wanted him to go out and join him there. When he came over here he could not get a job that suited him. So he became a stevedore for the money...he was one of the lucky ones, he belonged to the union and he was nearly always regular when there was

work...my father was a very studious kind of man, he had piles and piles of books, he was a great reader, especially where the Irish question was concerned. He never smoked but he always wore a smoking cap, blue velvet with gold leaves round it".

For some people the Island was only a staging post on a longer journey. The "Greek Gypsies" who arrived on Millwall in July 1886 by ship from Corfu actually came from Turkey, Greece, Serbia, Bulgaria and Rumania. It is likely that they were fleeing increasing repression of their culture and way of life by these European states. Amongst them were coppersmiths, builders and farmers, but their appearance, at once exotic and desperately poor, was against them, as was their scant knowledge of English. They stayed on Milwall long enough to be photographed (see picture) but they and their travel-worn tents were moved on by the police to Hull and across country to Liverpool, suffering assaults and abuse on the way before they were finally able to take ship to America and the promise of freedom.

The mass movement of Europeans towards America, often via the London Docks and the East End, appears to have left only a few traces on the Island. There are references to isolated families of Russian or German origin, some of them Jewish; a number of Poplar and Island shopkeepers with Germanic names were persecuted during World War One. This is evidence of individual migrations, but there is no sign of any large settlement by Europeans in Millwall and Cubitt Town.

A few Chinese sailors had settled in Limehouse before the middle of the 19th century. Up to the 1890s their numbers increased until the area became known as Chinatown. It had Chinese shops and clubs and its own Christian Mission. The Chinese community in Limehouse and Pennyfields kept its own language and customs, and this gave it a mystery and enchantment which were the source of many lurid tales, most of them without much foundation in reality, of opium dens and criminal gangs, though Bert Hiscott (born 1888) did record in his autobiography that: "On our way to school we passed the end of Limehouse Causeway, where the residents were mainly Chinese and sometimes serious fights arose among the various factions there".

Sailors of Asiatic or Indian origin arrrived constantly in the docks and while waiting for their ship to turn round, or to join another vessel, they stayed in the Strangers Home in West India Dock Road. Such "strangers" from the docks sometimes found their way onto the Island and Bert Hiscott, who described the area as "cosmopolitan", had one particular memory of sailors in his mother's shop:

"A Lascar seaman came in and was provided with a pair of thick socks - it was snowing. He later returned with a lot more seamen including one of evident importance and they all sat down on the floor and proceeded to buy, and put on, thick socks".

Whilst many people were drawn to the Island in the knowledge that there was a variety of work available, a minority were recruited for specific jobs. These included some of the corn porters in the Millwall Docks.

Strikes by corn-porters in the new docks had occurred in 1873 and 1874. The dock company determined to break the strikes by bringing in blackleg labour and in this instance, many years before the great solidarity of the 1889 dock strike, they were successful. Dorset, home of the Tolpuddle Martyrs, was notorious for the low wages paid to farm labourers and for the employers' resistance to unions. It was a suitable place for dock company agents to recruit a docile labour force accustomed to heavy work.

Mr Jones, who worked in the Lead Works

when he grew up, recalled the Dorset origins of his family: "I am a second-generation Islander. My mother's family were farmers, yeoman farmers and they lived down in Dorset and it was at the time when the Industrial Revolution was taking effect and the farmers were not getting a living. They were producing milk, which they skimmed, which they made into butter and it was never more than fourteen shillings per hundredweight. And my grandfather, who lived down in this little village in Dorset, near Dorchester and the Hardy country, he came to the conclusion that he couldn't bring his family up there. He had already, he had three children, born in the country.... it may have been four. And he had some relation who was a customs officer in the docks and he said, Why not come up to Millwall, to Cubitt Town? And he came up here...first they lived near Ship Street and then they lived in Manchester Road...I think there was

The main hall of the Strangers' Home in West India Dock Road, 1900.

four more in the family, I think there were eight children...it was in the 1870s".

In the Census of 1881 for Stebondale Street there were three families living at No.118, a total of six adults, and 15 children. The three husbands, aged 37, 45 and 29, had all been born in Dorset, as had two of the wives, the third being from Somerset. Two of the men, and one of the boys, worked in the Millwall Docks. James and Sarah Vincent had seven children. All five elder children, including George, aged 7, had been born in Puddleton, Dorset. The two younger children, Sarah 5 and Mary 3, had been born in the registration district of Poplar (i.e., the Island). James and Jane House had moved around a good deal before settling on the Island. James may have been in the army. Their children were born in Dublin, the East Indies and Woolwich, the youngest being 6 at the time of the census. On the other hand, James and Sarah Long had three children, the eldest being 7 and all born in Poplar. From the age of the children, and their birthplaces, it is clear that the families had arrived on the Island between six and seven years before the census, that is, in 1874 or 1875 - just after the strikes

The 1881 Census also reveals a youthful, active, crowded society, engaged in many diverse occupations

In the 16 six-roomed houses between Nos.107 and 122 Stebondale Street lived 152 individuals, an average of 9 or 10 persons per house. There were 31 families altogether, with an average of five members each. The largest family was at No.114 with 11 members, the most overcrowded house was No.118, with 21 inhabitants. Of the 152 people, 56, over one-third, were under 10 years of age; 26 were aged between 10 and 20; 49, just under one-third, were aged between 20 and 40. Only 21 were over 40.

69 individuals, almost half the total, were shown as having an occupation, and their occupations reflected the local economy. 25 were shown as "labourers", the catch-all word which meant they had no recognised skill or trade but "laboured" either in the docks or in one of the local factories or engineering works. Of the other 44, four were shown specifically as "dock-labourers" and there were 30 distinct occupations amongst the remaining 40, including: boiler-maker, hammer-man, potter, shipwright, foreman ship-worker, lighterman, house-keeper, greengrocer, corn-miller, iron moulder, rice-mill worker, policeman, sampler, seaman and bricklayer

The Island's growing population still represented all the regions of the British Isles, and new arrivals continued to bring to Millwall and Cubitt Town a variety of regional accents and customs, and of traditional and rural skills. Their new lives moulded them into urban dwellers, living at close quarters with each other in the grimy, foggy, noisy environment of industrial London, making new friends and establishing links with other families. As the century progressed some were drawn into new forms of social and political activity.

In contrast to the earlier period of industrialisation, the Island population was becoming less a mixture of social classes towards the end of the century. Fewer business owners and managers were living on the Island, and the numbers of skilled men as a proportion of the total working population, was also falling (Cole, 1981).

The view of the Island expressed in the 1890s by local clergy, who might be regarded as typically middle-class in their experiences and ideals, was that the Island was : "...dull, deadly dull."., and that it was : ... a city of desolation...badly lighted, astonishingly foul, inconceivably smelly, and miserably bare and lifeless..". though perhaps the Reverend Richard Free was having a particularly bad day when he penned this latter remark, and clergymen sometimes painted a black picture of the circumstances of their congregation in order to raise funds from rich benefactors. However, the fact remains that the Island was no longer an attractive place to live if you could afford to move away.

Many Island firms were family businesses, perhaps of two or three generations. This personal connection continued but by the end of the century employers and some managers could, if they chose, live at a distance from the factory, thanks to new forms of transport, both public and private. Many did choose to do so, as the Island environment became increasingly polluted.

A comfortable villa in the clean and spacious surroundings of Blackheath or Epping gave Island businessmen access to facilities which the Island lacked, and made it easier to mix socially with people who shared their interests. Marriage created kinship networks and cemented these connections. Frederick Duckham married Maud McDougall of the milling family, and ship-builder Alfred Yarrow was godfather to Alexander Duckham. All three families lived in Blackheath.

Jabez Binks, owner of the wire rope works, whose wife was from the Bellamy family, tank makers, lived in Bromley-by-Bow and the family had a seaside house in Clacton. J. Morton lived in Epping Forest.

The general trend was to move or settle in some nearby suburb but there was still a middle class, business and professional presence within the Island population up to the First World War.

Some teachers lived on the Island - the headmaster of St. Luke's lived in Strafford Street, and the head of British Street School moved into one of the new houses in Charteris Terrace in 1907. On the other hand, Mr Stokes, a revered headmaster of Glengall Road School in 1915, lived in Higham's Park.

Lawn House, Thomas Pitcher's substantial villa, became a Sailor's Home with beds for 50 persons for a brief period in the 1850s. It was then leased to William Arrowsmith, a steamship broker and owner. William, a Devonshire man, lived there with his wife, his brother Henry (also a

George Green School, East India Dock Road, about 1900. On the left, schoolmaster Mr Bloor. Third row down, second from right, James William Thompson, of Mellish Street; back row, second from right, Cecil Neville; second row, second from left, Eric Bloor.

broker) Henry's wife and five children, a governess and three servants. In 1868 the lease passed to the East and West India Dock Company and Lawn House was divided into two flats for the use of their principal engineer and his foreman, Edward Leonard, another Devon man, and Welshman John Deer.

In Island Gardens Joseph Stewart lived in Osborne House for a few years before his death in 1889. Other members of the Stewart family employed at the ship yard lived in Plevna Street and Roserton Street. According to Arthur Hubbard's recollections, after John Stewart's death Osborne House became home to Mr Allen, who owned the pottery "a few hundred yards further up the river, where the Fire Engine Station is now". Mr Allen was interested in medicine and Arthur Hubbard recalls "I can remember going to Osborne House for some mixture for whooping cough, years before (it became) Island Gardens".

Early owner-occupiers of Glen Terrace in the 1890s included Charles Bedford, partner in a stevedoring firm; Charles Lennox, engineer and James Smith, berthing master. Among the landlords were Francis Hole, a tailor of Fenchurch Street and Thomas Bowkett, surgeon,

of East India Dock Road. Later occupants included William Watkins of the steam tug company, and a music teacher.

We have seen how employers like George Brockley, James Dewar and Joseph Cook also lived on the Island in East Ferry Road and Glengall Grove. The Thompsons of the Cuba Street works lived in Maria Street, then Mellish Street and James William Thompson went to George Green's Schoool. Men who were necessarily directly involved from day-to-day in running their business, like the haulage contractors Middleditch, Davison and Huish, and Mr Hames, of Silver Terrace opposite the Lead Works, all lived on the Island at or near their workplace, as did people running "one-man" businesses, like blacksmiths and farriers, builders like the Peckhams of Pier Street, and dozens of shop-keepers and publicans.

The Olley family, who originated in East Anglia, owned two pubs at one time, the *Prince of Wales* and the *Pride of the Isle*. Family members helped to run the pubs and lived in the streets round about. Owing a pub or shop seemed to be one way in which a skilled worker might improve his circumstances. Maurice Sexton was a metal worker by trade and also owned the *Tooke Arms* and *The Islanders*. T.E. Wakeling was an angle-iron smith, had a shop and owned several leasehold properties. George Deeks was a cooper, owned a "wet and dry" fish shop in West Ferry Road on the corner of Spratley's Row and several houses on the Island. One of his daughters married George

The Olley family outside The *Pride of the Isle* public house, about 1912. The small girl is Marjorie Bessie Brewis, born 1905 in Alpha Road.

Leverett, son of a barge builder who also owned five houses in Mellish Street, another example of family, wealth and property uniting through marriage within the same social class.

The decline of highly skilled workers in the population was partly a result of deskilling - coachmaker Edward Saulter becoming a labourer in an iron works, for example, and there are many other instances of production which had formerly depended on skilled hand work becoming either redundant (as in coach-making) or mechanised, as happened in rope-making.

Another reason was that with the arrival of cheaper forms of transport, skilled workers, and also the higher grades of clerical workers, moved off the Island and lived where they could travel to and from their work by tram, by train or on foot and later, by bicycle. Some families moved away in order to better themselves or their children, or to bring their living accommodation into line with their "respectable" status as white collar workers, putting personal ambition before family and neighbourhood ties.

Engineer Arthur Hubbard married a girl from Poplar in 1892 and they lived in Manchester Road and Glengall Road, then Galbraith Street, but finally moved to Charlton because: "Our daughters were growing and at school. They gained scholarships which made it necessary for them to attend a higher grade school. The one

The Brooker and Granvell families about 1900. Back row, Harry Brooker, Flo Parrot, Jim Granvell and Bill Anderson. Middle row: Alice Brooker (nee Granvell), Mrs Granvell, Mr Granvell, Gus Granvell and baby Alice Anderson. In front: Lily Brooker, Willy Granvell, Florrie Anderson. The Brookers lived at No.2, Manchester Road, where they had a shop; they also kept cows on fields in East Ferry Road. The family emigrated to Australia before the First World War. The Granvells lived in Byng Street.

chosen was St.Olaves School in the Old Kent Road".

George Spruson, the white metal worker, bought a house in East Ham and moved off the Island in 1904. Some moved because they had found work elsewhere, like Mr Pearson's father, an engineer. The family moved to Rotherhithe: "...to be near father's work, now in the Surrey Commercial Docks".

Some people emigrated, like the Brookers, the family who kept dairy cows on fields near the Lord Nelson pub. They went to Australia in the early 1900s. Another family who emigrated in 1913 was the Brassetts. Harry Brassett, a carpenter, and his wife Jess, nee Margett, had many relatives in Stebondale Street and Seysell Street. The first Margett on the Island had been a soldier in the Grenadier Guards who settled here after being wounded in the Crimean War. (He told his children that the principle treatment for injuries was salt rubbed directly into the wound).

The Brassetts leave-taking party was driven to Tilbury Docks in, it was reported, the first motor charabanc to be seen on the Island. A year later they sent back a photograph of the whole family on the verandah of their new home in Sydney - a wooden house called "Millwall".

Many skilled workers, however, where not in regular employment and could not risk moving. Ship-repair had its seasons, and even with the support of trade union benefits, a regular income could not be guaranteed. Other work, such as construction engineering, also varied in its demand for labour, and while a regular workforce might be maintained, both skilled and unskilled labour was laid off when orders slackened. Workers in this insecure employment would hesitate to take on the extra expense of supporting a scholarship child, however gifted, and would also be more likely to remain on the Island within easy walking distance of possible sources of work.

Unlike the earlier period, when skilled work dominated Island industry in the iron trades and ship-building yards, there were now more jobs on the Island for semi-skilled and unskilled workers than for skilled workers. This made a difference to family incomes. There was plenty of work for girls and boys fresh from the new schools - though they risked being laid off again before they could earn an adult wage. There was also a great deal of both full- and part-time work for girls and women - they worked in food processing, rope making, sack and tarpaulin making, at the pram and mangle works, and in all kinds of production which did not involve very heavy lifting or did not require an apprenticeship in the skilled trades (from which they had traditionally been excluded). For men in irregular work, whether skilled or unskilled, the possibility of supplementing the family income by the wages of young people and adult women was a further incentive to stay on the Island, even though the wages earned might be only a few shillings.

In spite of Cole's findings that the Island was becoming increasingly impoverished and overwhelmingly working-class in this period, it is apparent that, although the very rich had moved away, their influence was still felt, and that Island society was still a mixture of poor and better off, containing many overlapping "communities". Bert Hiscott, son of a shopkeeper, describing Island life as he remembered it before the First World War, wrote: "During their leisure time, if any, the local tradesmen and many factory managers who lived on their premises, had to make their own amusement and quite a social community obtained, and most enjoyable times were had. We had concerts and swimming galas and the church were very active in this social life"

Local businessmen, like builders Thorne and Peckham, stood for election to the local Board of Works and the Borough Council which replaced it, as well as the bigger Metropolitan Board of Works and the London County Council. Local MPs were Island ship-builder Joseph Samuda and later, Sidney Buxton. The latter was a Liberal and took a personal interest in local conditions. He was involved in discussions to resolve the "Docker's Tanner" strike in 1889 and was present at numerous official events and ceremonies. He gave money to the building fund for a new Methodist chapel in Cubitt Town, when other donors were Alfred Yarrow, John McDougal, Joseph Cook and the Locke Lancasters.

Class differences were acknowledged. One way in which this recognition was expressed was in marriage. Shared experience at work or in business naturally led people to mingle socially with their own kind, where skills and status would be mutually acknowledged and common interests discussed - thus Mr Harry Trudgetts, grocer and provision merchant, hard working and energetic, was "well known amongst the businesmen and churchmen of our locality" (Arthur Hubbard).

A study of marriage registers for the period shows that not only did most people marry locally, they almost invariably married within their own class or, women married into a slightly higher social group. Thus a labourer's daughter might marry a stevedore, but the daughter of a stevedore, or of an engineeer/boiler-maker, would be less likely to marry a labourer. Where a marriage partner was not local, this more often than not happened within a wealthier social group, for example, amongst professional people such as Customs officials or teachers, people who had more oppoortunity to travel and meet others from different communities.

As families become linked to each other through marriage - and parents with several children could end up with in-laws in as many other families - local ties were strengthened and the supportive domestic and workplace connections deepened into another generation.

The familiarity which so many people remember from the early 20th century stems from these networks of social and marital relationships. The regular exchange of news and comment, which thrived on the intimacy of life in the crowded streets, gave rise to the popular memory that "everyone knew everyone else" - a notion which could be taken literally within each small locality. The positive side of this was that troubles were known and might be relieved by neighbourly help; the down side was that privacy was almost non-existent.

"Well, the people over the Island that I knew, you know, we all had open houses there. The doors were never shut. That's where they get the saying from: 'It's only me'. When we walked in we said, 'It's only me' and walked straight through". (Mr Sullivan, born 1905).

However, some doors were not so easily opened. Living closely as people did and with little privacy, differences of class and social status were deemed important, something to be jealously guarded. Maurice Sexton's grand-daughter, brought up by two maids in the big room over the pub, was "allowed" to buy winkles from the man who came round singing "Cockles, and mussels, and winkles, Alive-o". She recorded: "Our grandmother used to order the girls to boil these winkles and they were another treat we had. They were supposed to be rather low class, to eat winkles, but she always indulged us and let us have some winkles".

Mr Bensley (born 1900) described distinctions within the working class, distinctions which survived in spite of solidarity shown sometimes in labour disputes: "...the only people that used to go in the saloon bars were fitters and engineers and if an ordinary man, an ordinary man in the street, happened to go in the saloon bar of a pub, with

someone else, they'd turn and look down on them and say, 'What's he doing in our bar? We won't come in here no more'...that's how toffee-nosed they were".

But Mr Bensley saw the Great War as a levelling influence: "All the gentry and the people that used to be down here, the Victorians, the shop-keepers, they were all the moneyed people round this area, all got levelled out, you see, when they went into the army. It made no difference if he was a shop-keeper or a road-sweeper, they wanted you in the Guards, you went in the Guards; they wanted you in the Navy, you went in the Navy. It was a fine leveller".

11. Working Life 1860-1914

"When I was ten years old, my grandmother said to me -now, there was a strike on then, a dock strike on then - she said, There's going to be a midnight march tonight, sit up and I'll take you down to the bridge and see them. The dockers were getting fourpence an hour and they wanted an extra tuppence and the masters wouldn't pay it and oh, they kept them out a long time and they had this midnight march and they come up with all torches and I remember then I was ten years old...and they wouldn't pay it but still they had to give in in the finish".

(Mrs Sophie Anderson, nee Thompson,).

Mrs Anderson's recollection of the date of the famous 1889 "Docker's Tanner" strike is very accurate - she was born in 1879 - and her story neatly summarises the main points. The history of the strike is well known and it has been recognised as one of the great demonstrations of working-class solidarity of the industrial age. The strike marked another decisive step towards the organisation of unskilled workers, following the equally famous "Match Girls' Strike" of the previous year.

The 1889 port workers' strike had vigorous leaders who threw themselves unstintingly into organising, fund-raising and speech-making. Its chief participants were the many hundreds of desperate men, with equally desperate families, driven to that desperation by near starvation wages.

The General Manager of Millwall Docks reported on the condition of casual workers in 1888 (one year before the strike) that

"...the poor fellows are miserably clad, scarcely with a boot on their foot.. they cannot run, their boots would not permit them...there

Unloading coir at Millwall Dock, about 1914

are men...who come on without having a bit of food in their stomachs, perhaps since the previous day; they have worked for an hour and earned fivepence; their hunger will not allow them to continue; they take the fivepence in order that they may get food, perhaps the first food they have had for twenty-four hours".

As details of the conditions under which they lived became public, sympathy for the strikers grew, helped along by the dignity of the dockers' marches and by the support of other port workers.

The Manifest of the General Strike Committee was signed by officers of the Amalgamated and United Stevedores on behalf of "the whole of the dock workers of London - stevedores, painters, scalers, corn porters, deal porters, coal heavers, ballast heavers, wharf labourers, shore gangs, donkeymen, seamen and firemen, carmen, lightermen, bargemen, derrick hands, hydraulic crane drivers, tug men, etc., etc".

With this support and that of the Australian dockers, the strikers were helped out with funds and were able to keep the strike going. Public figures like Cardinal Manning became involved

on their side. Eventually the dock chiefs gave in and sixpence an hour became the basic rate.

Relations between employers and port workers remained fraught and there were other, less successful strikes in the years before the First World War. The basic rate had improved but because of the uncertain and highly labour intensive nature of the work and the competitive structure of the port, the casual system remained in force throughout the docks.

Shipping could be delayed by fogs and stormy weather or held up in other ports. When ships did arrive it was in the interests of the ship owners and the dock companies to unload and reload quickly and this was where casual workers came in, taken on as and when needed to supplement the permanent men. A regular work force was maintained in every dock but demand for casual workers varied with the cargoes handled and the traditions which had developed.

Hydraulic cranes were in operation, but in the main cargoes of all kinds, whether in bulk or packaged in barrels, cases, sacks or boxes, were literally man-handled out of the depth of ships' holds onto barges and to shore and into warehouses, or vice versa; were raised, lowered, heaved, shoved, shovelled and barrowed by sheer muscle power, augmented by the docker's hook.

In the dock offices and warehouses all the detailed records of individual consignments, their movements, sampling, checking, handling and storage costs, were made by hand or typewriter when these became available and in the absence of telephones, messages were taken round the docks between warehouses, offices, ships etc., on foot. There were categories of worker for every conceivable job and type of cargo.

The Millwall Dock Company had a relatively large permanent workforce by comparison with the East and West India Dock Company, because special skills were needed to handle the grain and timber which were the main goods handled in Millwall Dock. Here is part of a list from the Millwall Dock Company Establishment Books for the 1880s and 1890s:

"...book clerks; paylist clerks; paymaster; junior/senior clerks; messenger head/assistants; ledger clerks; ship inspectors; stokers; shunters; engine drivers; firemen; cleaners; drivers; berthing foremen; transporting foremen; foremen greasers; shipwrights; carpenters; first, second and third class foremen; overhead truckmen; tippers; hatchwaymen; cranemen; backers;

DOCKERS CHILDREN WAITING FOR BREAKFAST
IN WEST INDIA DOCK ROAD

spoutmen; tyers; weighers; levermen; nozzle hoppers; grain samplers; shipworkers; doormen; tubmen; dock master; deputy dockmaster; assistant dockmaster; gatekeeper".

It was reported in the 1880s that the Millwall Dock hands were: "superior to the ordinary dock and waterside labourers" because they were "countrymen...cut off from the social influences of the East End... as a rule they belong to some religious organisation and are united together in clubs and benefit societies...the whole work is let out to large labour contractors (who) live near their work and associate freely with their men. Each master has a small permanent staff of labourers, guaranteed one pound a week".

Agnes Matthews' father came to the Island with his parents as a little boy, when his father was offered a job "to work for Mr Cubitt":

"After he left school, because - things weren't very good in those days and my dad could have gone on to train as a teacher but the father couldn't afford to keep them on at school - and then his father died very young so it meant they had to go to work. So he went into the docks and he worked in the docks all his life. He was a ship worker actually...he was given a ship to load and he had to plan where they're going to load the goods onto the ship and the different parts they go into. He worked for Maltby's in the old - in Millwall Dock.

And where the pub is, where the George pub is...they used to go out of a morning and they'd all stand - he wouldn't but the men would stand on what they called the stones and just wait to be called for a job. And then they used to have what they called a ganger, that took on the men, he'd take on twelve or thirteen men, and he'd just stand there and choose who he wanted out of them. And that's how they were employed. That's casual work, you see. They'd probably be taken on that day until the ship finished and then they'd be out of work unless there was another boat ready to come in".

Robert Morris, born in Saltash in 1862. Migrated south and worked all his life in the Millwall Docks. He took part in the 1889 Dockers' Tanner Strike. This photograph was taken on the 50th anniversary of the strike and was published in *The Daily Worker*.

A trade union gathering in Poplar, about 1890.

Other eye witness accounts testify to fighting as the men were chosen and to the custom of buying drinks for gangers in order to keep in favour with them.

The labour intensive nature of dock work was mirrored in all the other workshops, factories and lesser enterprises around the Island, some of which also employed casual or seasonal workers.

Bert Hiscott, born 1890, was employed at Mortons throughout his working life (like many others Islanders) and here is an extract from his autobiography:

"At the Millwall factory although there was a recognised daywork rate for each employee, there were thousands of straight piecework rates for most of my time. The staff at one period reached to 1,600 hands including casual labour, but as mechanisation came along became less, it got down to 700 people". (There was little mechanisation before the First World War).

"The peak period of the year was of course the fruit season and it was strange how the Bush Telegraph seemed to know when the fruit was expected which would need picking over, that is, plugging strawberries, snibbing gooseberries, strigging blackcurrants and so forth, and queues used to form at an early hour outside the factory gate for this poorly paid work.

In 1902 regular hands got say ten shillings a week of fifty-two hours for adults, women, and say, twenty-five to twenty-eight shillings for daywork, adult men. The casual rates were lower, and were tuppence an hour for women and sixpence an hour for men. Some casual women had tuppence ha'penny an hour for sticky work like boiling peel.

Pieceworkers could of course earn much more than the day work rates. I think some skilled women workers who made "variegated pipe" could make about two pounds ten shillings per week but they had to be trained a long time to be proficient. A man packer who slogged might make three pounds.

I will try and remember a few of the thousands of piecework rates, and may I be forgiven if they are a bit out: "wheeling on tops onto tins of hot jam" - one penny per gross; "rolling and kneading melted sugar to make boiled sweets" - one shilling per hundredweight".

Casual workers were paid as the job finished and, as wages clerk, Bert often had to stay on late to settle up. This had its compensations since: "...one foreman had a pleasant habit of bringing in a peck of strawberries for me to sample". Strawberries weren't always enough to keep Bert at his post though: "...one night I quite forgot that I had some (fruit workers) to pay and as I had a date at Blackheath, I shot off there and they had to go home without their pay. When they came up next day for it - and some had to walk a mile or so from Poplar - I said, where have you been, I've been waiting here all night for you. They were very good and took it all in good part".

There were other workers who demanded - and received - cash on the spot. This included the skippers of incoming steamers:

Island working men, before the First World War. Back row: George Fothergill (he and his brothers worked in the docks, probably as stevedores); Alf Perry, steelworker; George Glasson, who lived in Steboncake Street; Bill Fothergill; Bill Lavender, who lived in Manchester Road near Cubitt Town School; Tom Fothergill. In the front row: Bill Crabbe, a painter and decorator with Stocker and Roberts; George Chamberlain; George Peake, b.1864, a riveter at Westwoods; William Peake, b.1885, also a riveter, worked at the London Graving Dock, travelled abroad building bridges in his youth and lived at No.60 Manchester Road; Bill Bonnet, a train guard from Walthamstow.

"...immediately he arrived he would present himself at the office for his freight charge, required in spot cash. Another man who demanded cash as the job progressed was the steeple-jack who repaired the tall factory chimneys. He explained that he first paid his casual labour, then his men, then his old woman and last the rent. He lived in a small house in a poor district and I don't think the tax authorities got much out of him. Boiler scurfers also had to be paid as the job progressed".

Low pay and long hours were found everywhere - in factory work, home work and shop work:

"I worked in Maconochies and then I went across the water to another factory and I used to get up at 6.30 in the morning and walk through the tunnel right round the waterside and be in work by 8 o'clock. Sometimes it would be 7 o'clock before I finished work... it was a cement factory and I used to sit and sew them bags, to hold cement, by hand. I used to have seven-and-six a week, give my mother five shillings, and with the other half-a-crown I used to put a shilling in the club to buy my clothes". (Mrs Skinner)

The rope trade was classed as a sweated industry. Wages at this time ranged from twenty-eight shillings a week for rope-makers, to ten shillings for spinners. Women mill hands received nine shillings a week, all for a 54-hour week, daily from 6.30 am to 5.30pm with half an hour for breakfast and an hour for dinner; the works closed at 1.30pm on Saturdays. Women walked from Canning Town to work at Hawkins and Tipsons, their worn boots wrapped in sacking in snowy weather.

Mill hands from 'B' Mill, Hawkins and Tipson's Globe Rope Works in East Ferry Road (the site of the present Mudchute DLR station). Photograph taken before the First World War. The men are Frank Harding and Charlie Lay.

Island women took in home work, perhaps not in such quantities as the box makers and paper bag makers of Stepney and Whitechapel, but under similar conditions:

"At one time my mother took on a contract for about 200 bonnets for the workhouse and my brother and I, outside school hours, had to carry these in large card boxes up to the institution at Poplar. I believe the price was one shilling and threepence each and all labour and material had to be provided by the maker. How my mother managed the long shop hours, housework, cooking and this contract I do not know but I suspect she worked far into the night".(Bert Hiscott)

He records shop hours then (1897) as "until ten o'clock on week nights (except on Thursdays) and to midnight on Saturdays, and people often knocked on Sunday morning for something which they had forgotten".

Arthur Hubbard's first job on leaving school aged 12 in 1881 was at Harry Trudgett's grocery shop in Cubitt Town. The long hours (before eight in the morning until after ten at night and midnight on Saturdays) meant that one of his parents always had to wait up for him. This was tolerable until Mr Trudgett acquired a pony for his rounds, and the feeding and watering of the pony on Sundays also fell to Arthur. So at the age of 14 Arthur moved on:

"My next employment was with my Uncle at a barge building works at Orchard House, Blackwall, rather a long walk night and morning, but my evenings and Saturday afternoons and Sundays were free for leisure and pleasure, something I was not able to get while at the grocers".

Before the 1880s many children had no schooling at all and when it finally became universal and compulsory they still left at 12, though for many this had risen to 14 before the First World War. Child labour was therefore entirely accepted as a fact of life and only parental concern stood between children and harsh conditions, low pay and long hours, conditions which have become familiar to us through the novels of Charles Dickens. As in many homes their small wages were a welcome addition to the family income, parents did not often intervene. It was adult workers who were likely to protest at any introduction of cheap juvenile labour into their traditional tasks.

Mrs Anderson said: "When my father did grow up, he was put in the iron works, rivet-carrying for boiler-makers; as soon as they were able to hold, take hot rivets out with the tongs, they could get a job, the boys could. Never mind about whether you were 14 or not, soon as you could handle anything without dropping it, and old mother Cutler, their old mother, she used to stand at the forge as well as us rivet boys, you know, working the bellows for the hot rivets...the Cutlers, oh, they died millionaires, almost. Stingiest place to work..".

John Pearson started work in 1903 at the age of 14, in a solicitor's office:

"Hours nine till six, one o'clock Saturdays, for six shillings per week. This frequently meant seven o'clock before being on my way home. Travelling expenses, a weekly ticket on the Great Eastern Railway to Fenchurch Street, were one shilling and sixpence. I was given a place in the "fair copying" office where three men worked. They did nothing but this fair copying day in and day out, earning twenty-eight to thirty shillings per week. They would augment this by taking on similar work for stationers, which they took home...they wrote most beautifully, particularly their copper-plate on parchment. Although I was supposed to finish at six, a batch of letters was daily handed to me at that hour for hand delivery round the City area. This frequently meant seven o'clock before being on my way home".

It was not the long hours but the mannerisms of one of the partners that led John to look for another job: "The senior was jovial, blunt but sometimes disgusting with his language. He was hardly a nice man. I was terrified of him, but felt scornful on discovering he used a jerry which he kept in a cupboard under his desk! His nickname for me is too unpleasant to mention. Another illustration of his beastliness was his occasional interspersing of foul words when dictating to his clerk, who was a tiny little man and most capable".

One way in which harsh conditions were lightened and a little laughter was brought into the work place was through the practical jokes and pranks which people played on each other, using whatever materials were to hand. Apprentices were normally subjected to initiation ceremonies which could be quite rough and tumble, or of a subtler kind like being sent for "a long weight".

Another bit of light relief was the annual outing, a traditional event looked forward to all year round. Before paid holidays became standard this was often the only day away from the Island that people had and they made the most of it:

"On Saturday last the employees of Messrs Brown and Lennox celebrated their annual outing. A four-horse brake started from the gates at 9am sharp. The musician accompanying them was beyond reproach, except for a severe shortness of breath. They arrived at the *Carpenter's Arms,* Thornwood Common, at about 1.30 and here a substantial dinner awaited them. Dinner being over, they adjourned to the forest, after which a concert took place. Mr Toot Martini presided and the songsters were Nat Wallis, Darby Roach, Clarence Suffragin and Digger Budd... Wells and Wells gave a burlesque entitled *The Coster's Holiday,* and were ably supported by some of Messrs Wright's girls (from the rope factory at Millwall, who chanced to be pretty near on their annual outing)....After this, *Auld Lang Syne* was sung and the excursionists took their places in the brake to start for home. They reached Millwall about 11.30pm, after a very pleasant time of it". (From the *News and Chronicle*, 18th September 1903).

Laws about working conditions were very few and it was difficult to enforce them. Comforts and amenities of even the most basic kind were often lacking in factories and docks. Maconochies new factory in 1897 provided nowhere for the workers to shelter while they ate their dinners. Office workers were allowed little freedom. When Mr Morton died, it was recorded in his obituary that: "he had an army of young clerks in his office and it used to be said that they were not even allowed to go out of the office to wash their hands without getting a written permit, made returnable in a certain number of minutes, which were not be exceeded by a second". though this may be an extreme example. In many workplaces there was nowhere to wash. People got dusty from flour or cement, grimy from oil, sticky with sugar, and went home - dusty, dirty, grimy and sticky.

From photographs we can see how closely together people worked and how little protection

Boiler-makers at work in Yarrow's ship yard, before 1900.

there was from heavy machinery, hot metal and other potentially hazardous substances. Bert Hiscott said that workers in Morton's wore gloves when cutting tin plate because of the sharp edges, but health and safety precautions were minimal and accidents of all kinds frequent. Compensation or benefits for the family depended on the good will of the employer or on membership of a trade union. There were no standard or state benefits other than an appeal to the Poor Law Guardians.

When Mrs Flowers, of Laura Cottages, West Ferry Road, lost her husband in 1882, she was awarded a gratuity of ten pounds by his employer, F.A.Hughes, lighterman and barge builder, of Deptford Ferry Road. Mr Hughes had six pounds in hand owing to Mr Flowers, perhaps accumulated benefit, since this paid for his funeral. Out of the ten pounds, Mr Hughes paid seven pounds, eighteen shillings and threepence for a mangle for Mrs Hughes and gave her the balance in cash. There is no record of how Mr Flowers died but since his employer was generous it may have been in an accident at work. Mrs Hughes was set up for independence in widowhood, with her mangle.

"At the age of about 50 my father had an accident in the wire factory, when lifting one of the large bobbins of wire strands that made the great ropes for the ships. He could not work any more because he could not draw his breath. He could not get up from his wooden armchair, it would take his breath away. There was no compensation in those days, though for two years I went to the factory and was given five shillings a week from what they called the slate club for which I presumed my father had paid while at work". (Lily Cain, born 1897)

The diver's job was one of the most dangerous in the docks and this is reflected in the relatively generous terms of the employment contract offered by the dock companies at the end of the 19th century. When George Henry Shaw was engaged by the Millwall Dock Company in 1898 his wages were fifty shillings for a 48 hour week, with overtime pay of two shillings and one penny per hour. He was to reside on dock premises and to have a total of 14 days paid holiday. If sick, the first 13 weeks would be on full pay, the next 13 weeks on half pay. Charles Pearce, the diver he replaced, who had retired, was given a pension of thirty shillings a week.

The diver is an extreme case but illustrates the point that skilled workers had better wages than

unskilled and semi-skilled workers, as long as they were in reasonably regular work. They still laboured long hours in dirty and dangerous conditions, but more and more, by the end of the century, skilled workers enjoyed the protection and support of their trade unions.

Union activity increased by leaps and bounds during the half century before the First World War. By 1907 there were 37 branches of different unions in Poplar, including not only the skilled workers and stevedores but unskilled workers as well, and the unions had been instrumental in founding the Poplar Labour League, forerunner of Poplar Labour party, in challenging the dominance of Liberals and Conservatives in local politics and in helping to get socialist Will Crooks onto the London County Council and eventually into Parliament.

In 1904 the Poplar Guardians decided to give outdoor relief to the unemployed instead of taking them into the Workhouse, as they had done up to then. This money came out of the local rates. The rates went up, ratepayers grew annoyed and formed the Poplar Borough Municipal Alliance in protest. The Alliance called for, and got, a Committee of Inquiry into the conduct of the Guardians. The Inquiry found that Will Crooks and George Lansbury, the two people who had taken the lead in the new policy of outdoor relief, could not be criticised for their handling of affairs, though they may have been more generous with the rates - "extravagance" was mentioned - than was strictly necessary.

Because of their relatively high incomes, skilled workers were well-placed to have nation-wide networks of well organised, branches. These "new model unions" as they were called, of the skilled trades, were established from the 1850s onwards and the first trade union congress met in the 1860s. New legislation made it easier for them to operate and when urban working men got the vote in 1867, political alliances were formed between the Liberals in government and the new trade unionists. Later in the century these alliances gradually broke up as the parties realised their opposing interests and as the prospects of having labour representation in Parliament improved.

The Isle of Dogs Progressive Club, founded in 1897 and with its own premises in Pier Street (see picture), was an organisation typical of the fluid political situation of the time. Not radically socialist in itself, the club supported Poplar Labour League with an annual donation of ten pounds. Will Crooks, Poplar Labour member of the London County Council, attended the club's opening ceremony. The Club also had the support of local businessmen like John Peckham, a builder who lived in Pier Street. He allied himself with the interest of working men and small-scale entrepreneurs, against the larger Conservative interests. There was no Labour candidate for Cubitt Town in 1903 and John Peckham rightly considered he had a good chance of getting the socialist vote. He got through with the highest number of votes, 693 more than Conservatives Fred Thorne (another local builder) and Colin Gordon (who both lived in Blackheath) with 628 and 648 respectively. All three were elected to the Council, while the other two Progressive candidates trailed behind with 466 and 457 votes each.

Elections in those days were lively, even wild affairs. Sidney Buxton was Liberal MP for Poplar from 1886 until 1914. The Liberals were defeated in 1900 but Sidney was returned again in Poplar and Mildred Buxton wrote in her memoirs: "...it was thrilling; as we got near to Poplar Town Hall, the crowd got larger and larger and more and more came rushing up and we could hardly get inside the Town Hall, the crowd was so excited, yelling and bellowing with joy...the result was shouted from the balcony, Sidney made a little speech of thanks and everyone bellowed and sang and screamed until they were hoarse. They insisted on taking the horses out of the carriage and dragging us about a quarter of a mile to the Liberal Club".

Boiler makers, engineers and carpenters were amongst the skilled trades who formed strong national unions from mid-century onwards and all three were well represented on the Isle of Dogs. Arthur Hubbard, who learnt his trade at the barge works in Orchard Place and at Westwoods, was admitted to the Boiler Makers and Iron and Steel Shipbuilders Society in 1889 at the age of 20; "...for being a member of a Trades Union, I had a better chance of obtaining work at any firm who catered in ironwork and shipbuilding, also there were some benefits such as sick, superannuation and out-of-work allowances, payable according to years of membership".

Arthur eventually became branch secretary of Millwall No.5 branch:

"In this direction there was plenty to do, attending meetings, paying out benefits, receiving

Islanders gathered for the ceremony of laying the foundation stone of the Isle of Dogs Progressive club in Pier Street, on July 3rd 1897.

contributions, conducting the correspondence of the branch. Every Friday evening the unemployed, sick and the superannuated received the weekly allowance and on Saturdays fortnightly contributions to take. Then the general business meeting on Thursdays took up a good number of hours weekly. There was also a monthly return to send to the General office in Newcastle, giving account of expenses and state of trade, a quarterly balance sheet to make out and audited by the branch auditors, giving account of income and expenditure for three months. At the end of the year the General Secretary required an annual balance sheet...so that an annual report could be printed and sent to every branch in the society.

I liked the work and became interested in keeping accounts. Also there was a small salary attached to the office which was handy, especially when work was slack.

Arthur was branch secretary of his union for two seven years periods, from 1895 to 1902 and from 1912 to 1919. His brothers Dan and Albert were also union officials, of Amalgamated Engineers, and Carpenters and Joiners, respectively.

12. Domestic Life

Long hours, low pay and dangerous, dirty conditions, - no wonder the thousands of men and women looked weary as they tramped the streets homeward.

They left work tired and dirty, walked home as often as not in rain or snow or smut-laden fog. In his article in *The Builder* in 1901, the Reverend Richard Free said some Island workers spent up to an hour walking home. No wonder that people employed in low-paid jobs lived on the Island in overcrowded conditions, to avoid the walk to work and the bridges, the ferry or the tunnel, as they could not afford the luxury of a horse-drawn bus.

Home at best was crowded and for some was just one room shared by all the family. It might be cold and cheerless or hot and steamy with washing drying round the fire and suet pudding on the boil. It was smelly and alive with bugs. There were no such things as bathrooms but there might be running water, one tap in a shared scullery or back yard. We can only marvel at the effort that went into turning a family out in their Sunday best in conditions like that and sympathise with those for whom it was too much of a struggle.

Poverty was very evident on the Island in this period. Booth's survey of the 1880s, quoted in Cole, recorded that over 43% of the Island's household's lived in poverty. This compared with 34.5% for the East End and 30.7% for London as a whole. Other records of the time, as well as remembered experience, confirm the details of the circumstances in which nearly half the Island's population lived.

The Reverend Richard Free of St.Cuthbert's church, in his book, *Seven Years Hard*, (1907) reported that an income of twenty-four shillings a week (48 hours work at sixpence an hour) was insufficient to keep a family of six. Detailing the weekly outgoings, which amounted to about twenty-nine shillings, he pointed out: "...obviously something is wrong with the poor man's housekeeping. He will have to eat less bread or pay less rent".

There were many families where a regular income of twenty-four shillings a week would have seemed a luxury. though some had more. Mrs Choat remembered that : "...my father earned thirty-two shillings a week and my mother kept us all on it, four brothers and one sister and we never had margarine only butter or our bread or else good beef dripping".

In *Nights in Town*, Thomas Burke (c.1900) gave an idea of the food budget for a working-class family on the Isle of Dogs:

"Little Elsie is here too, buying for a family of motherless brothers and sisters...two penn'orth of pieces from the butcher's to begin with (for tuppence you get a bagful of oddments of meat, trimmings from various joints, good nourishing bones, bits of suet)...then to the large greengrocer's shop for a penn'orth of "specks" (spotted or otherwise damaged fruit and vegetables of every kind). Of this threepen'orth the most valuable is the bones, for these, with a bit of carrot and potato and onion, will make a pot of soup sufficient in itself to feed the kiddies for two days. Then at the baker's you get a market basket full of stale bread for twopence and at the grocer's, two ounces of tea, two ounces of

The Lloyd family in the doorway of No.7 Samuda Street in 1908. At the back, Mrs Rosie Lloyd with her sister (or possibly a neighbour). The children are Olive Lloyd (later Foster, who worked at Hooper's marine cable works); Rosina, who died at the age of six; Florrie; Ernie, who worked at McDougall's; Alf, who also worked at Hooper's, Fred, who worked in the London Graving Dock. When Olive was older she worked as a cook in the Tooke Arms public house. Several members of this family died when Samuda Street was bombed in September 1940.

margarine and a penn'orth of scraps from the bacon counter for Dad's breakfast".

Dock strikes drew attention to the dreadful circumstances of dock workers' lives - especially those casually and occasionally employed, as opposed to the permanent or preferred workers.

"Deaths from starvation are, unfortunately, only too common amongst dock workers..". This quote, from "The Docker" in *The Workers' Daily Round*, Watney and Little, 1910, seems extreme but is confirmed by a coroner's report of 1906 in which it was recorded that a man, formerly a labourer, had died of starvation in Cubitt Town.

In 1889 it was calculated (by Seebohm Rowntree) that the barest minimum upon which a family of five could survive was twenty-one shillings and eightpence. The cost of living rose in the years leading up to the First World War, and so did expectations - workers were no longer satisfied with the bare minimum of existence. They wanted newspaper, clothes, a social life, better eduction for their children and meat more than once a week.

More than one Islander remembered not so much their own hunger, but other children's: "Over Millwall, right up that way, you know, as you are coming down from West India Dock Road, and at Mortons, the big factory there, the kids used to stand outside with no boots or stockings on and "Please, have you got any bread.".. before the First World War, when I was a kid, I'm talking about".

Barefoot children were seen in the streets partly because boots and shoes were so precious: Mr Sullivan, born in 1905, recalled: "I went to St.Luke's School and if we had a pair of shoes on at school when we came home from school we all had to come home and go to Mum and say, Mum, I am home from school. Right, take them boots off and go and play out in the street. With no boots on, I am not telling no fairy stories".

On the Isle of Dogs in the last three decades of the 19th century and the years leading up to the First World War, there was so much casual work, so much seasonal work, that family circumstances could vary widely from week to week. So many other things affected a family's earning capacity - strikes, accident, illness, old age and death. If there were several adults earning, this was comfortable - but if they were out of work, they still had to be fed. If there was only one breadwinner and he or she could not work for any reason, disaster immediately loomed. No group of workers, from the highly skilled boiler-makers to the casual day labourers,

were immune to this insecurity, although skilled workers were more likely to be cushioned against poverty by trade union benefits. This is the background to the workers' campaigns for better wages and working conditions, and to the long struggle to get representation in Parliament.

When work stopped suddenly, the pinch was felt at once. John Pearson, born in 1889, was only three when he: "sensed something amiss. There was not our usual big meals...fried bread for breakfast! Lots of stews instead of meat. Bread with a little sugar. We were feeling the pinch. It was because of a strike in the engineering trade".

In these uncertain circumstances an allotment, or some rabbits or chickens kept in the back yard, or a little help from friends and neighbours, could make all the difference .

David Thompson's youngest son, Alex, born in 1895, explained: "...my father was a boiler maker, but then, in them days, he hadn't got no regular work. Sometimes he might be working for three weeks and other times, probably only two days, or two weeks, probably he'd be out of work three weeks. Well, when he was working, you had steak. When he wasn't working you had bread and butter...and everybody had, in their gardens they had chickens, rabbits, and when things were a bit hard, you'd go out and kill a rabbit, or go out and pull one of your chicken's heads off. No, you never starved".

George Pye, born in 1909, whose father was a stevedore, had his first experience of poverty during the dock strike in 1912: "We used to go into church and get a bag of pea flour to make soup...the old man used to keep chickens and he had to kill these chickens and they was his pride and joy, but he had to kill them, for us to eat".

Keeping pigs in urban areas came to be seen as a potential health hazard and was banned early in the century. Before that, some Island people kept pigs but a family did not eat a whole pig. The carcase was sold on and everything edible was of use. Kate Whiting, whose father kept pigs, recalled:

"When the pigs were killed - because he used to keep pigs, he kept everything that was eatable - if he wanted his pigs killed, we had to go down Stebondale Street, there was a butcher's in Stebondale Street, and we used to have to go and get him to come and kill them....we sold it to live on, cos our father was an invalid. We used to have to take it round the pubs. There was a woman along here, she was poor, and she would say to me, "Your Dad doin' any pigs, fetch us in the tails". They wasn't much, but they was a dinner, you know".

Meat was doled out carefully in Kate's household: "My father came from Bristol and my mother came from Newcastle...and when we sat down to dinner our father would say - because we always used to have our pudding first, always had a suet pudding with jam on, you always had that first before you had your dinner - he used to say, them that eats the most pudding will get the most meat. Well, we used to stuff ourselves with pudding just to get the meat!"

John McDougall had rented land from the Millwall Dock Company in the 1890s and let it out in allotments. Ben Thomas, born in Limehouse in 1900, wrote that:

"...most of the Millwall residents had the allotments, but some men who rented them came from Poplar and even Limehouse and it was quite a common sight to see a man on a bike coming off the Island loaded up with a variety of vegetables such as potatoes, cabbage and brussel sprouts, carrots and parsnips".

Money lenders and pawn shops were used as ways of raising essential cash and were regarded as a necessary evil. Mrs Anderson remembered: "Old Bridget, who used to stand and wait for men to come out of work and shout: "Oi, what about that shilling you owe me!".

John Pearson wrote that: "..a Sunday suit or dress was a necessary part of all wardrobes. The ladies were tight-waisted, with leg-of-mutton sleeves and very high collars. Men wore high starched collars..top hats or bowlers were another adornment..". But other recollections record that innumerable Sunday outfits went to the pawnbroker on Mondays to help the family through the week, to be reclaimed the following Saturday ready for wear on Sunday again.

Lily Cain, whose father died when she was 15, explained how they managed:

"My brothers were working, my mother did washing and ironing for the people that could afford it, at three shillings a dozen and a shilling a dozen for mangling only...On Monday mornings our Sunday special clothes were carefully ironed, our boots and shoes were cleaned and the boys' Sunday suits were ironed also. These things were packed in the parcel and sent to the pawn shop a little way on the left on the other side of the road. My mother was too proud to take the parcel herself but a woman used to call and take it for her for tuppence and bring the money for us to live on, until Saturday when the men got their wages and we took the old pram and went to the pawn shop for our parcel, taking the money and the interest that was charged".

Kit Viera's father was a crane-driver in the West India Docks and got to know ships' captains, who: "...used to be invited back to the house for a cup of tea and a chat..". To keep up this social life and a facade at least of well-being, it was still necessary to use the pawn shop: "Mother had a nice fork and steel and mother used to take that and they used to give her two shillings for that and she used to get it out, always got it out at the weekend".

The pawn shop and the money lender meant a vicious circle of continuing debt unless good fortune struck and the family could break the cycle of borrowings and repayments.

Local loan clubs and savings clubs were a better option for those with enough money coming in weekly to put a little away, Mrs Skinner's mother held things together with a mixture of economy, the support of a relation and saving. She had eight shillings a week to buy food for a family of ten:

"She was a good manager, we always had a good dinner every day...my mother had a sister, she wasn't married, but she was in service in Scotland and more or less she helped us to buy our clothes...Mr Wallace used to come round on a Tuesday afternoon, and I think she used to save sixpence. Then we used to have a loan club, she used to pay a

Sophie Anderson (nee Thompson, born 12.8.1879 and died in 1982) with her husband Harry (born 5.11.1872 and died during the Second World War) photographed in 1899, a week after their marriage. They lived at 251 West Ferry Road, where Sophia's grandmother took in washing from families who lived in houses at the Pier Head - divers, dockmasters, pilots, etc. Sophia fetched and carried the washing and also turned the heavy mangle, weighted with stones. Grandmother took in lodgers too and this is how Sophia met Harry, who came from Warwickshire. His father had been a railway wagon inspector, and Harry was a boiler-maker.

shilling every week and that would save up for Christmas...used to run one up the *Ferry House*, they used to have to go up and pay it...".

The savings were worth while. Winifred Davey remembered:

"Christmas was a wonderful time for us young ones. Everyone came to Grandma's for Christmas dinner, sharing the cost. The front room was cleared of as much furniture as could be and at dinner time a trestle table was erected. The men were in the scullery doing the washing up and we children were given our dinner first, the women doing the serving in the kitchen and bringing it to us, dirty plates being given to the men. When we had finished we went up to our flat to play quietly while our parents had their dinner. In the evening with Aunt Grace playing Grandma's piano and with all the older ones singing and dancing, it was grand. Living near everyone went home in the small hours to sleep".

Everyone worked at whatever they could. Hop-picking, pea-picking and fruit-picking were country harvest times which Island people, especially those with connections in Kent and Essex, returned to again and again as a ways to supplement the family income. When schooling became compulsory in the 1880s it was difficult to persuade parents that mothers should give up these working holidays when they coincided with school term. St. Edmund's School log book for 15th July, 1881, contains the following record:

"...the attendance for the week was only fairly good. Some of the children are in the country, pea-picking and fruit-picking. Some of the girls in the highest standard are coming irregularly just now, their parents keeping them at home to help in the house work".

They may have been kept at home to look after infants because older sisters and mothers were all working in the jam factory, it being the busy season for soft fruit. This casual work continued as long as Morton's could use the extra hands. Mrs Anderson said of the years at the turn of the century: "A lot of women went out to work, leaving the children bread and butter and a drink of water for when they used to come home at twelve o'clock and cook them a dinner when they used to come home from work. There used to be Maconochies, there used to be a jam place, then there was a sack place over Millwall Dock bridge..".

It was normal for people to help each other in many different ways, such as feeding each other's children, lending goods to be pawned and adopting motherless babies.

Islanders, like working people everywhere, struggled against poverty with a kind of nobility and self-sacrifice not expected today.

George Hames related a story told him by David Thompson:

"Before he was superintendent (at Cutler's) he was just a normal workman and he was not at work and he heard there was a job going at Kendall Green Gasworks. Well, he walked from Millwall, and he walked from Millwall to Kendall Gasworks, that was in Ladbroke Grove, and got the job. Before he left he had sixpence, that's why he walked. He left that with his wife. He had half a dozen kids and when he got home there was a hot meal waiting for him, they had all had a hot dinner and she hadn't spent the sixpence, she had a ha'penny left out of it, that was before 1914, he told me that himself".

This story illustrates the multitude of husband-and-wife partnerships which kept children fed and families out of the workhouse where they would have gone without the hard work and strict economy seen here.

Resort to the workhouse was a last act of desperation. At an earlier stage in the decline into absolute poverty, families might be given food, which Mrs Sinclair recalled as : "parish food, hard bread and big lumps of meat, all rotten, it got dark and we would go and throw it over the park, it smelt and we wouldn't eat it...you had to go and fetch it in the High Street, Poplar, in the old workhouse...'.

Hunger was a frequent guest at their table. She went on: "We would go home (from school) and we would find no dinner. And never had a dinner at school. Went to work hungry and come back hungry, yes".

In her family it was the mother who worked to feed the children: "she would take in a bit of washing to earn enough to buy a loaf of bread and a bit of meat...downstairs, in the scullery, an old copper, you would have to go out in the back and take a candle out because she would be washing out there when it was dark, to get the washing done to get the money".

There was nothing to spare for extras such as a second set of underwear:

"Saturday, my mum used to say to us, now I haven't got the money to buy you any underclothes, you will have to stop in and let me wash what you've got on. Yes, washed and dried and ironed, she said, and then you can go out. So we had to stop in while she washed and ironed, washed dried and ironed them. Not only me but my sisters an' all. So that we could all go out clean".

A few fragmented words of recollection are in most cases all that is left to record the hard work and sacrifice of so many mothers:

"She used to work at the school; and she used to do a bit of nursing, she used to follow Dr Cardale.

The Jenkins family of 63 Galbraith Street, in 1908. At the back, Fred; Violet, who married Frank Gentry and lived in Galbraith Street; Maud, who married Fred Burdett, of Poplar and later lived in Dagenham; Benjamin, whose first wife, Eva, died young; he re-married and settled in Kent.
The children in front are: Grace, who lived in Galbraith Street when married; William, who also lived in Galbraith Street and worked for the Alexander Tug Company; Ada, who married Alfred Stevens and kept a draper's shop in Marshfield Street.

He used to say, Go round and book up with Mrs Thomas, she'll look after you. And she used to take in washing. She worked hard, my mum did. I remember her standing in the scullery twelve o'clock at night with a few candles on the ledge, washtub there, washing away. But she never drunk, never drunk nothing. See, my dad used to sometimes, when he'd done his own work, he used to say to her, Penny on the table...send one of the children round for half a pint. But she never drunk, she used to put a drop of cold tea in a jug, make out she'd had a drink. She'd say to us, Go round and get ha'porth of titbits for her, and ha'porth of sweets in three papers for the three littlest - titbits, liquorice allsorts then". (Daisy Clayden, nee Thomas)

In the docks and factories of the Island, great quantities of raw materials and finished goods passed daily through the hands of thousands of poorly paid and often hungry people. Naturally some items found their way into pockets and down trouser-legs and away home to be eaten or sold. Bert Hiscott said of the docks that: "...pilferage used to occur at the docks and it was said that to those in the know, many goods could be obtained. Hearsay had it that when lefts and rights of shoes were sent separately, even then pairs could be obtained. Tobacco which hadn't paid duty was also known to be about".

Mrs Choat went to work as a young girl at the Star Pram and Mangle Factory in Cubitt Town and recalled: "...old Mrs Fudge, she taught me my trade there. She never wore a coat, always an old cape, and the things that went out of the gate under its cover was nobody's business. The gateman never stopped her, he knew her so well".

Better-off Islanders, usually the women, helped the worst off. Mrs Fuller's grandparents were George and Eliza Deeks who owned the wet and dry fish shop in West Ferry Road:

"There were many people living in poverty and my Grandma Deeks used to make large bread puddings and take them round to needy people. On one occasion she found a German family, parents and two children. The parents were in bed suffering from bronchitis and the children were so hungry they were eating the linseed from the poultices which had been laid on the parents' chests. Also I remember my Mother telling me that when the fish from Billingsgate was sorted out, the small fish which were unsaleable used to be put out into a

Mrs Eliza Deeks, of Millwall, 1842 to 1922. The Deeks were staunch Methodists.

bucket which was placed at the open shop door and poor families could help themselves and according to my Mother the offer was never abused".

Elizabeth Dew recorded similar stories, handed down through her family, about her Grandmother who: "...used to take soup to people. There was an old soldier who had come back from the Boer War and he had an Indian wife. He shook all the time and his wife had become paralysed...My Grandmother took soup to them and there was another family of Russian Jews my Grandma took soup to. Mum remembers them as being very timid".

Winifred Davey (born 1902) remembered Mr Chappell, the caretaker of St.Luke's School: "He was a very kind man who collected trimmings from the butcher and greengrocer and whatever else he could get, to make into soup which he gave to those children whose fathers were out of work".

It was a humbling experience to need the help of the local middle class in this way, even more so to have to go, effectively begging, to the church or other charitable institution, or worse still, to the Poor Law Guardians with their miserly hand-outs. At the turn of the century socialists councillors like Will Crooks and George Lansbury did a great deal to improve conditions in the workhouse and the way in which poor relief was distributed. It was still regarded as the last resort.

To avoid such sorrows through independence and self-sufficiency was a matter of pride and there were hundreds of working-class families on the Island who, through a combination of hard work, good fortune, judicious marriages and good management, maintained a relatively comfortable standard of living. The way a woman ran her home could make a crucial difference and many people refer to their mother proudly as having been "a good manager". It was to avoid the worst of poverty that many older women exercised strict control over their sons and daughters, in supervising their personal lives and in training them to "manage" well. Jean Parmenter wrote about her grandmother, Clarantania:

"I remember how she organised her tribe of great strong men, her precise instructions from the old wooden armchair in the kitchen to her daughters concerning their household duties. Mrs Beeton's household words were nothing compared with my gran's utterances.....Gran's sons gradually brought home sweethearts for her inspection and then disappeared into the surrounding cottages to set up their own families, not far away and still within the supportive ambit of their mother-in-law, who was always ready to help in any tribulation. The daughters did the same, always closely controlled by mother, who saw that they mixed with "nice" young men who never got drunk or bet on the horses".

Gran also withheld the customary wedding present (a pair of double blankets) from a niece who became pregnant whilst engaged to be married.

The community neighbourliness and family networks were strong but they did not take care of everyone. Living close together as people did, the consequences of drunkenness, illegitimacy, and family breakdown for whatever reason, were all too well known. Children's homes, in Forest Gate and later in Shenfield, and the workhouse in Poplar

Robert Mitchell Dewar and Kate Elizabeth (nee Hallett) with their sons Frank, Victor, Robert and Harold, of Plaistow, and formerly of 49 East Ferry Road, photographed about 1906. Robert senior travelled the globe as a chief engineer. Robert junior was killed in the early stages of the First World War.

High Street, sheltered the victims of some of these misfortunes,

"My mum had a very, very sad life, you know, her father was an old seaman and he wasn't very good to his wife and my mother had brothers and years ago they were put in homes and all that".

Frank Soper was left an orphan in his early teens and none of his older married siblings would give him shelter. He spent the night in Spitalfields market and the next day although under age, enlisted in the army.

The lives of the better-off who lived on the Island were very different. Maurice Sexton's grand-daughter, born in 1892 and brought up in the large living-room over the *Tooke Arms* in West Ferry Road, where she was cared for by two maids, remembered going shopping with her grand-mother:

"When my Grandmother went shopping she went to the end of Commercial Road and there was a great store there with a big teapot outside where they sold tea and currants, raisins, sugar loaf and some of the sand sugar. I used to have to sit on the chair, which was a very tall chair with a cane seat. I was plonked there and there I had to sit while they ordered their things. The tea was in a great big cannister with a little lid and the scales were two pans which went up and down. Grandma bought black tea, Indian tea and green tea which I think was China tea. Of course tea was very important in those days, very expensive too. I can see the man now, holding the scales and balancing them and she bought a pound of this tea and a pound of that, out of these big cannisters".

A boiler-maker and engineer by trade, Maurice Sexton had an active business and social life. The Sextons also ran *The Islanders*, a smaller pub in Tooke Street, (sometimes known as "*The Sextons*"). Maurice Sexton and his wife knew many of the ships' captains who sailed into the East India Docks. They and their wives, together with some of the more important passengers, were often entertained in the large dining rooms at the rear of the Tooke Arms.

George Brockley, who owned a copper works and lived in Launch Street, left the following items in his will when he died in 1904: books and bookcases, a bureau, framed portraits, a diamond pin and silver snuffbox, an American eight-day clock, a mahogany chest of drawers, a suite of bedroom furniture, one easy and three cane-bottomed chairs, an American organ and sewing machine, two silver watches, diamond and gold rings, plate, glass, china, linen and pictures.

The factory owners in their distant homes lived in another world altogether. Alexander Duckham wrote in his autobiography:

"...those years at the turn of the century now appear quite nostalgic in recollection, personally as also nationally. We were all residing around Blackheath, spaciously and comfortably, with large quiet gardens and wonderful service. Carriages for parents, bicycles for the rest of us. Billiards, music and whist in the evenings, with home dinners and dances at frequent intervals. How very static and assured it all was".

13. Social life and Leisure

One of the greatest changes to come about in Island life in this period was the arrival of free education for all. It kept children out of the workplace until they were 12 and gave them a new world of their own, with the prospect, for some at least, of a wider choice of jobs when they left.

However, it took some time to be accepted, partly because the first new schools charged a small fee.

Mrs Anderson went to school in the 1880s: "Well, they were ever so strict, still, we had to have schooling. They stopped us taking the money to school and sent a big fat man round to collect it, 'cos the mother used to say, Well, I give my son or my daughter their tuppence to take to school, so if he didn't pay it he must have spent it. So they stopped us taking it to school and he used to come round collecting it. Oh, it was a stern old bloke, I can picture him now, strolling along with a big book under his arm, he'd knock at the door and say, I can't keep waiting here. Oh, he used to get some saucy answers an' all".

There were other reasons why children stayed away from the new schools - including the need to care for young siblings whilst mother or father was at work, or a lack of boots and other suitable attire. Hence the efforts of the "School Board Man" as the attendance officers were known, and the fines imposed on parents of persistent offenders.

Once schooling was established as a part of the life of every child, many children accumulated happy memories of lessons, teachers and outings. Classrooms were crowded and discipline strict, but overcrowding and severity were only what most children were accustomed to at home: "When they said No, we knew they meant it and the cane never did us any harm. It made you have self-discipline because you would not let the other children see you cry and you didn't get it unless you deserved it. If you went blabbing home to your parents they would say, If you had behaved yourself you would not have been caned. If it had been for something really bad your parents would punish you as well".

Childhood was short - they could leave at 12 to start work and so the freedoms and pleasures of schooldays stand out in the memory of many, although not everyone appreciated the cane.

Arthur Hubbard recalled the delight of his first days at the new Glengall Road School in 1875, where "everything was clean and new". The lessons included grammar, geography, singing, freehand drawing, model and geometry, literature, physiology and drill.

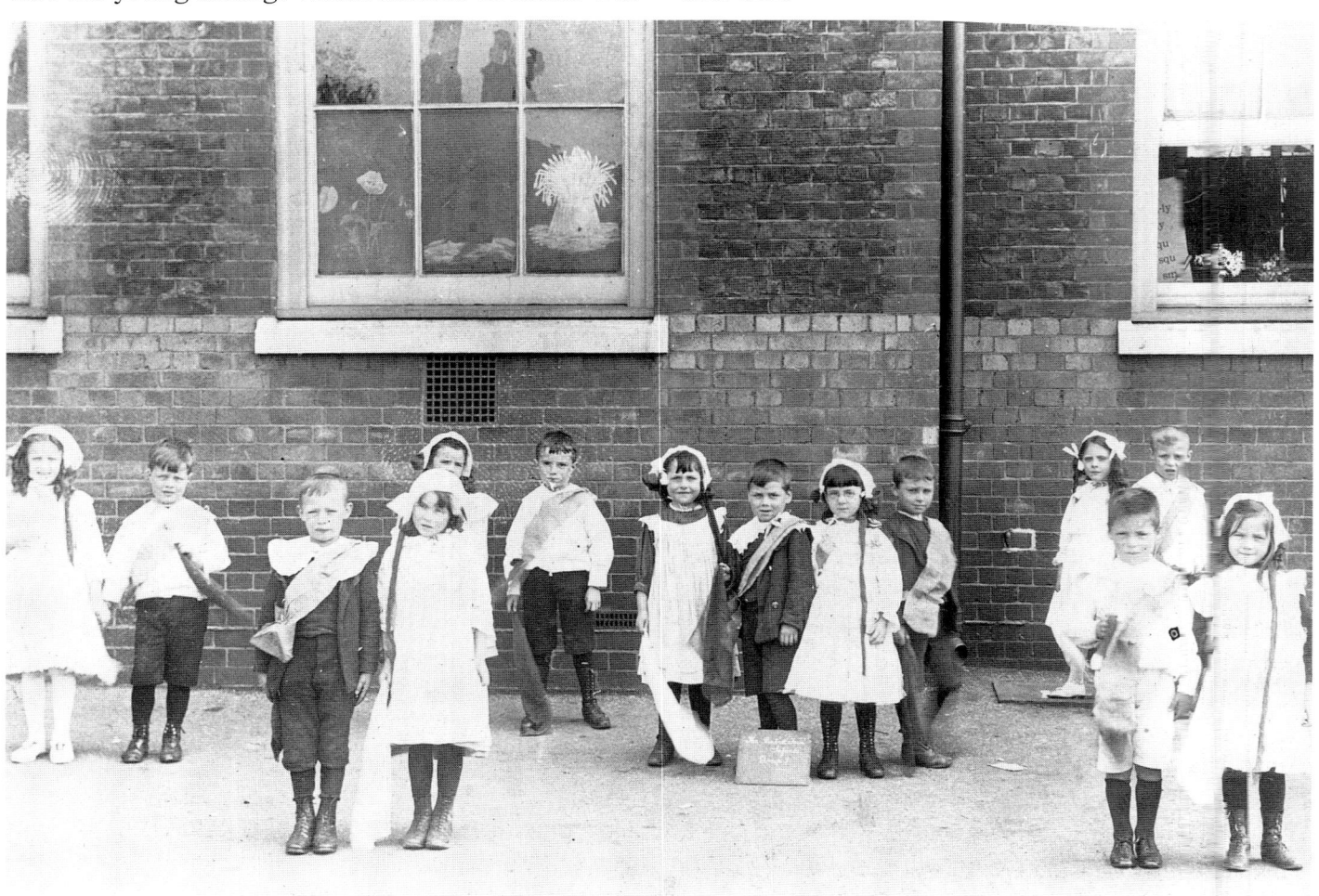

Eileen Saunders, born in 1905, could remember "...no problems with learning or behaviour..." but "There always seemed to be something to look forward to....memorable school events were celebrations for May Day and Empire Day. On May Day, the girls were in their prettiest dresses with wreaths in their hair, and we would dance round the May Pole. A May Queen would be chosen and would 'sit in state' surrounded by her attendants. On Empire day a King and Queen, who had previously been chosen, would be presented with gifts from groups of children dressed in national costumes. This would be followed by songs from England, Ireland, Scotland and Wales".

George Daniels went to Millwall Central School when it opened in 1906. One of the teachers was a Mr Barter who: "began to take some of his class for country rambles into Kent and Essex on Saturdays. He organised a week's trip at Easter to Brecon in South Wales. We were taken by horse-drawn brakes to Paddington, thence by train to our destination where we were accommodated at a small hotel. We had several excursions in the neighbourhood...The following year we went to Dolgelley in North Wales where we climbed Cader Idris and went over the gold mines in that area where the gold for our present Queen's wedding ring was mined".

For some children even the journey to school was an education. E. Greenaway, born in 1904, said: "The Island was a wonderful place for children to live. We had to cross the Millwall Dock Swing bridge and could watch ships from all over the world loading and unloading. We knew the flags of all the countries and knew the shipping lines by the emblems on the funnels. I remember the blocks of sugar and huge locust beans with a vein of sugar running through them. How we got to eat them I don't know".

Religion, like education, imposed new restraints on children and also opened up fresh and enjoyable worlds.

Arthur Hubbard's father was Sunday School superintendent at the Cubitt Town Methodist church for 50 years and Arthur said his Sundays, when the family went three times to service, were "happy days". The activities which Arthur recalled were common to most Sunday Schools on the Island and in most cases continued well into the 20th century.

"We looked forward to the Sunday School Anniversary, singing special hymns...parents made

Cubitt Town School before World War One.
This school was on the site of the present St. Luke's in Saunder's Ness Road.

this the opportunity for putting on the children their summer clothes, the date being the third Sunday in May. The tea and public meeting on the following Monday, was an exciting time...Another joyful occasion was the Sunday School excursion to Epping Forest, by brakes and vans...perhaps the longest ride by vehicle that many children had during the year. The London Sunday School Festival at the Crystal Palace was another red letter day....all the schools in London participated..... 5,000 singers had to attend eleven rehearsals, six local, three district and two of Mr Hinton's (the conductor) which took us into Poplar or Stepney. it was a magnificent sight to see 5,000 singers seated on the Crystal Palace orchestra...The year 1880 was the centenary of Sunday Schools and the Festival that year excelled all others in joy, gladness and excitement".

Besides the Sunday School, every place of worship laid on other activities for both adults and children - Band of Hope, Mothers' Meeting, Boys' Club, Men's Club. Members of each congregation organised concerts and plays, set up football and cricket teams, and held outings, bazaars and Christmas parties. St.Edmund's Church had a gymnastics club for girls on a Monday evening, boys on a Tuesday evening and the boys and girls met on Friday evening to dance. Every year the gymnasts competed against other East End Catholic clubs at Caxton hall.

St. John's Church had a particularly full and flourishing programme of activities for men and boys, described by John Pearson (born 1889) in his autobiography:

"The vicar and the two curates were a wonderful team who stayed together for many years...(and) held together a fine congregation. There was a club house for men, also a boys club, in addition to a flourishing Boys' Brigade... a big choir of men and boys, perhaps one of the best in the East End. There were practices for the boys every Tuesday evening and for the full choir in church on Fridays. The organist and choir master was a Mr Gardner (on the staff of the Bank of England). He was a musician to his finger tips and got the best out of us. The choir boys had an annual treat of their own, normally to a theatre in the West End. The men had a supper. I do not think any community could have lived through a happier phase than was ours at that time..".

In 1892 Winifred Davey's grandparents moved to a new house at 52 Alpha Road, where her parents also lived and where she was born. She went to St. Luke's School and St. Luke's church, where her father was in the choir, like her uncle Jack, who also lived in

Alpha Road, and her other uncle Arthur Crane, father of the violinist Arthur Crane. She recalled the united effort that went into building a new church hall:

"Everyone on Millwall worked to raise money for the Parish Hall. A Miss McQuire, who was a good amateur actress, directed and produced "HMS Pinafore". It was a wonderful show, performed in the school with a stage built by the men of the choir. Most of them took part in the production.

Local firms were also very good about giving money and at last the new hall was built. It meant badminton on weekdays, whist on Fridays, dancing to Arthur Crane's band on Saturdays and Sunday School on Sunday afternoon".

Listening to music and performing music were activities which were part of Island life for almost all adults and children. Whether it was bawdy ditties in pubs, or sacred hymns in church, it cost nothing to sing and gave great satisfaction.

Traditional folk songs were learnt at school, hymns at church or chapel, and the popular songs of the day were heard in the music halls and sung round the piano at home at impromptu parties or in the public house - or without a piano if necessary.

John Pearson, who regarded himself as "one of a typical working-class family, five boys and three girls; my father was an engineer", remembered family life:

"Aunts, uncles and cousins always seemed to be visiting. There was great fun round the piano, except on Sunday evenings when Mother insisted on 'sacred music only please'. One of my older brothers was really clever playing the piano by ear. There were times when Mother queried his rendering of Sunday's sacred music. Dad occasionally played hymns at her request though he too did not play from the music sheet".

The music halls on the Island, in big rooms on the first floor of public houses, had gone by the 1880s, but the *Queen's* at Poplar was a venue where well-known stars like Marie Lloyd made occasional appearances. Talking about one of the songs Marie Lloyd used to sing, Mrs Anderson said: "One of my brothers sung that song, when they heard a song like that they would sing it all the time for weeks and weeks".

"Lots of people had pianos" according to one woman. Those who had no piano went round to someone who had, or the piano was brought out into the street. There was a room for "entertainment" in all the social clubs of the era - this usually meant a concert, often performed by local talent.

Errand boys and others could always be heard whistling in the street, often the popular songs they had heard in the music hall.

The street was where outdoor games were played, away from the restrictions of church, home and the workplace and was full of the possibility of pranks and adventures for boys. (Wet or frosty weather kept children indoors, playing on the floor, under the table or on the stairs anywhere out of the way of tired or busy adults).

Street "roughs" were a constant feature of Island life in this period. Thomas Wright noted them in the 1860s. A letter to the *East End News* in 1877 complained that they gathered on the pavements outside the *Glengall Tavern* and the *Lord Nelson*, spitting, cracking nuts and harassing the passers-by. The well-intentioned Richard Free was persecuted by "roughs" during his efforts to bring Christianity to the poor of Millwall. He conducted his first service over a background noise of cat-calling, coughing, jeering and more nut-cracking from lads who had invaded the premises.

Mrs Anderson, born in 1879, recalled from her youth: "...the roughs, what they called the roughs, who didn't care whether they went out in rags or what..".

The street was a market place for the many traders who came round selling their wares - muffins, shellfish, milk, bread, vegetables, cat's-meat; there were gypsies with pegs. The street was a theatre, there were organ-grinders and street entertainers. At certain times of year the street was thronged for the processions of the Catholic Church, sacred but colourful, enjoyed by all denominations.

The street was the place where illegal bets were taken, the arena in which a long-drawn out battle between public and police was conducted, usually in a permanent state of armed truce: "They had what they called a bookie's runner and they used to stand on the corner of the street taking the betting slips, see? Then the police come along course, they've got to hop it, haven't they? They knew, the bookies knew, when they were going to be pinched. Because lots of times the police would turn a blind eye, but then they'd tell them. They'd say, 'Now, we're going to nick you next time.' And they probably would. They'd go to Arbour Square there and they'd get fined, probably about a fiver".

The street was also a place for gossip, for overseeing daily life. On warm evenings it was usual for adults to sit outside rather than in their overcrowded homes, watching children at play and taking note of any unusual activities. Drunkenness, quarrels, pregnancies, courtships, new clothes, any kind of misbehaviour, were all observed and subjected to comment.

Mrs Choat recalled that Jack Olley's cart was "a meeting place for gossip". He sold green-groceries and her husband, when a boy, was employed to "put the nose-bag on the horse and keep him still when he got fidgety because ...sometimes it would be 11 o'clock at night before he finished his round".

The streets were rarely quiet, since pubs were open until midnight and shops till ten or eleven at night, the flaring lights of gas or gentler glow of paraffin lamps casting shadows over the pavements.

The shore and the river drew the boys and young men, in spite of, or because of, the dangers. The shore could yield riches; mudlarking was still a worthwhile occupation. Bits of metal collected on the shore could be sold in bucketfuls to scrap dealers round the Island. Oddments of timber were converted into firewood for use at home or sold for pennies.

Boys played on the barges, occasionally with tragic consequences. They learned to swim in the river - it was free, unlike the new public baths in Glengall Road and in Poplar, but East End sport historian Colm Kerrigan considered that free access to the river encouraged swimming as a sport. It received a further boost when the London and India Dock Swimming Club was formed in 1894 to promote swimming, life saving and water polo, using both public baths and the dock waters.

The "Club and Messengers Championship" was held at the West India Export Dock on an August evening in 1904. Ben Thomas witnessed such an event as a boy and described it as : "..an exciting time. It was held in a dry dock, which was half filled with water from the river Thames. The seats were formed by the high steps of the dock. The races were of the full length of the dock, half length, over stroke, side stroke and back stroke, besides breast stroke and half a race doing one stroke then changing to another stroke in the next half. A lot of men and boys went to watch, besides a few women and girls".

Cricket was a traditional Island sport, with clubs first appearing in the 1860s and with a training ground on the streets. "Early tuition was often with a lamp post for wicket and budding wicket keepers generally used their coat instead of gloves and pads. (There were) one or two very good local teams despite pitches almost devoid of grass". (Pearson) The letter-writer of 1877 complaining about "roughs" had a further grievance, which was that "cricket and other games are carried on every Sunday on the open space near the *Lord Nelson* and no one interferes". Some firms had their own teams, Yarrows was one, and Yarrow's Cricket Club met for their first annual dinner in *The Queen Hotel* in 1880, with George Brockley in the chair. Alfred Yarrow was president of the club whose members appear to have been his skilled employees. Formal club membership with annual fees and other costs was probably out of reach of poorer semi-skilled and labouring men.

It cost next to nothing to kick a ball about though and football was the Island's great game by the end of the century, quite how this began is uncertain except that it was probably part of a national trend. The Island's professional team, Millwall, is said to have originated with the works' team of Morton's factory, and they played on the Island until 1910, with gates of 5,000 being common. Several Islanders recall the crowds tramping down East Ferry and Westferry Roads towards the ground on a Saturday afternoon. Kit Bradley was born in 1900: "I remember them, Saturday afternoon, traipsing along, from Poplar and Canning Town, all walking down to the football ground, all walking to see a football match. I remember that from a child until I was about 10. "

The east side of the Island was a breeding ground for great players. East End sporting historian Colm Kerrigan cites St. John's and Glengall Road Schools as producing some particularly fine young players in the 1880s and 1890s, some of whom went on to become professionals. John Pearson, who attended St.John's in the 1890s, tells of the mania which gripped Island boys:

"Most of us played football and if a proper ball was not to be had one was made up of rags. Anything would do to kick about. ...games would often be before breakfast, when daylight permitted and at every conceivable opportunity throughout the day. We were football mad..".

Kit Bradley could remember an individual footballer, Jack Calvey:

"He was a stevedore, but he played football for Millwall. He lived with us for a time and in fact he got married from our place. He married a girl, she lived in Poplar, she was the prettiest girl, she was really beautiful. He used to drink, you know, in fact he sold his international cap for a pint of beer, in the *Magnet*...and he was one of the nicest men

Millwall United 1898-99. In the back row: W. Doughty, T. Lawrence, H. Collings (capt), A. Goby, A. Hockley (secretary), G. Cooper, J. Brown, H. Topping. In front: G. Collins (trainer), T. Hoskins, R. Barry, H. Baillie (vice-capt), A. Sutherland and W. Bell. The original belonged to Len Ball, whose aunt appears on the left - she helped with teas at the match.

you could meet. His favourite song was "Poor Jock of Hazeldene". It's an old Scots song, he wasn't Scots, he was Irish, of Irish descent. I heard my mother say that he was a wonderful son to his mother. He used to write regularly to his mother and send her a few shillings. He was on the refined side. You wouldn't think he was a labouring man".

In 1901 the club moved from their original site in East Ferry Road as the ground was needed by the Millwall Dock company (it became "Transporter yard"). The new ground was at "North Greenwich" on what is now Millwall Park. It was a grassy, water-logged field, which had to be steamrollered to level it before the first match, a game against Aston Villa, could be played. An old shed was used as the players' dressing room and to start with, water had to be carried to the ground in tubs.

With a professional team of players as role models it is not surprising that every place of work, every pub, every church, chapel and other institution, had its own football team, sometimes more than one. This enthusiasm left an enduring legacy on the Island.

Other popular sports held on the Ivanhoe Sports Ground in West Ferry Road were athletics and dog racing, for which, one newspaper article noted: ..".there is a big demand, for the Islanders, many of whom are from the North, dearly love their dogs".

Boxing was practised in most boys clubs and there was a dedicated training club next to the *Millwall Dock Tavern*. Like football, it offered a potential way out of poverty into the glamour and riches of professional sport.

These are all sports for men and boys, building muscle power and keeping them fit for the hard labour of their daily work. There was apparently little organised sport for girls outside school, though girls also went swimming and cycling. Walking was probably their principle form of exercise, often pushing a baby in a pram or handcart and they were generally engaged in training for their role in the scheme of things - minding younger siblings or neighbours' children and helping out at home, at least until they went to work at 12 or 13: "My mother used to knit all the socks for her brothers and woe-betide her if

The Millwall Dock Tavern and Hotel, about 1900. The boxing club was in the premises to the right of the picture. "Lion Packings" was a local company, based in Garford Street. The pub was located in West Ferry Road, near the Millwall Dock entrance, outside the present West Ferry Printers gateway.

she was caught reading a book. She said she was always either knitting socks or rocking a cradle". (Mrs Fuller, nee Leverett)

Many sports clubs were attached to public houses or held their meetings there and public houses were important centres of social life throughout the century. Pubs were meeting places for the Foresters, the Buffs, and various sports clubs, savings clubs, social clubs, workingmen's clubs and co-operative societies, as well as trade union branches. Homing pigeon societies had their headquarters in pubs and quiet games of dominoes, shove ha'penny and darts were played. News about possible work was passed round in pubs, and gangers or foremen were treated there. As there was a pub every few hundred yards, everyone lived within easy reach of a "local", and all but the most dedicated abstainers used them to a greater or lesser extent, both men and women.

According to the Salvation Army publication, *All the World*, in 1892, Island pubs had earlier been notorious for their "Judge and Jury" clubs. One former adherent, who had frequented the *North Pole*, explained: "We used to swear in a policeman

and a jury and we used to try all sorts of cases". The writer alleged that: "...not only the sailors but the numerous dock labourers, the navvies, factory hands, and even tradespeople in responsible positions, would enter upon drinking bouts and orgies that made night hideous and scenes of brutality frequent".

The truth behind these lurid words may never be known. It has to be remembered that the article was written to promote the temperance movement. In spite of the appeal of their brass band, The Army's open-air services were frequently broken up with violence, the flag torn and instruments smashed in the 1870s and 1880s and a meeting hall in Glengall Road, Cubitt Town, had to be abandoned after two failed attempts to get a congregation together. One reason for the continued failure of the Salvation Army to set up a permanent Corps on the Island may have been its unpopular attempts to persuade adults to stop drinking, although in the Methodist chapels the Band of Hope and Temperance League attracted many members.

Another view of a pub night out is a newspaper report of a meeting of the Ancient

An Evening Continuation School outing from Millwall to Kent, the original of this photograph had the following names written on the reverse: B. Hiscott, Fisher, Rayne, Doe, Newton, W. Palmer, Keithing, G. Doe, L. Ward, Moyce, Bone, E. Barham, W. Goldstein and B. Hunt. Bert Hiscott went to the evening school and met his future wife there.

Order of Foresters in the *Lord Nelson*. Numerous toasts were drunk, including the health and prosperity of "Court Cubitt", songs were sung by the Island Amateur Christy Minstrels and the party "separated in the small hours, highly pleased with the proceedings".

Drunkenness was not uncommon. Mrs Anderson recalled a husband and wife who regularly set about each other on the pavement outside the pub on Saturday nights. She talked about: "...one called 'old Barbara', she used to come in the Prince, she'd get drunk, three o'clock

when they shut, she'd come out, singing, old Scots woman she was, she fell down in the gutter, one day, pouring of rain, her husband let her lay there till five o'clock".

Other people have remembered Saturday night fights and the sight of the drunks being taken away on a wheelbarrow to cool off. Alec Thompson (born 1895) when asked if women drank during his youth, replied: ' Oh, yeah. Women - they had - dinner times and all. Night times, dinner times, they were in there till half past twelve, twelve o'clock at night. Singing their heads off and - 'cos it only used to be tuppence a pint of beer then, in them days, you know, and whisky used to be threepence a drop. And what a drop - about twice as much as what they get today. They had them (children) in there on their laps, suckling them in there and probably you'd see them, half a dozen, asleep, little kids..".

The appeal of the pub lay not only in its social function, but in the fact that here, in a warm, bright, jolly atmosphere, accompanied by workmates and friends, the bone-weary worker could forget for a short time the anxieties of home and the hard labour which awaited him or her the following day.

Feminine refinements were in short supply amongst the hard-working factory hands. Maconochies women were noted for settling disputes with their fists (George Hames) and the rope works girls were "real toughs" (Bert Hiscott). Drunkenness amongst factory women and girls was an aspect of Island life which distressed the middle class women who founded St.Mildred's Settlement in 1897. They reported that: "Drink Clubs were held in many of the factories, the girls putting in a few pence a week, each to get a bottle of spirits to be drunk on the premises before breaking up for the holidays (whiskey was then three shillings and sixpence a bottle)".

They tried to combat this practice with "Supper Clubs" and the award of a red flannel petticoat, a strategy which was successful and "...in a few years Drink Clubs (at any rate on the Island) were a thing of the past".

Strong-minded wives prevented their husbands from consuming a week's wages at the bar in one go by waiting for them outside work on pay-day. Children were aware of the problems, since some older people recalling their childhood take pains to emphasise that "mother didn't drink", though they were generally tolerant of a father drinking, if it wasn't to excess. The churches, chapels and Sunday Schools campaigned constantly for abstinence or at least moderation in drinking.

By the end of the century society was in many respects less brutal and violent than it had been 50 years previously. Sunday Schools, the temperance movement, the trade union and co-operative movements, the prospect of representation for working men in Parliament and perhaps above all, universal education, had given rise to new interests and new ideals. Libraries, cycling clubs, cheap rail fares, competitive team sports, church choirs and evening schools offered wider horizons and alternatives to bare-fist fighting, illegal betting and late night drinking, though these pastimes still flourished. In 1911 the Reverend Merrilees of St.John's Church reported that although in general: "morality was good, drinking amongst women was on the increase".

Bert Hiscott said of the new library in Strattondale Street that it was "a great boon to the Island...introduced us to new literature and caused me to haunt the second-hand bookstalls and to acquire cheap editions of Dumas, Haggard, Hood, and I picked up an unabridged edition of Sales 'Koran'. Bert and his friends went cycling: "Our favourite run was to Birchwood Corner, Kent, where our programme was to pick bluebells, in the woods, or later in the year, blackberries, then a slap-up mid-day meal at Cleavers the butchers, then a good tea and back home in the evening".

Winter entertainments were different: "During December and January most of the young people managed to attend eight or ten parties at each other's houses when games, dancing and ballad singing, often till as late as four o'clock in the morning, and many a time I had much ado to keep my eyes open at work at the office next day. I remember after three parties in succession we tried to dance a set of Lancers on Westcombe Park Station, whilst waiting for the first early morning train, and on another occasion I was sitting in the middle of Blackheath, about midnight, playing a mandolin".

Bert wrote with a dry humour, appreciative but without nostalgia. For many Islanders, the years before the First World War have been remembered in the light of what came afterwards, giving a specially rosy glow to childhood memories of peacetime and simple pleasures:

"I remember when Alpha Road was asphalted everyone saved to buy skates and in the evening Alpha Road was full of people skating. Our Nell hurt her ankle and that was the end of her skating, so she gave them to me. I loved skating but the War in 1914 ended many things that were good.

My daughter once asked me if I had a happy childhood because, she said, you often talk about it. On reflection I realised that in spite of all the drawbacks (WC down the garden, bath in front of the fire, very little money) I did have a happy childhood. We all lived near relations who were always willing to help and all our neighbours were the same. You felt secure in love and kindness, which was wonderful". (Winifred Davey)

1915, Raglan Barracks, Plymouth. Albert Conn is at the back on the left.

14. One Soldier's War

In 1914 the rivalry between European states, which had been intensifying over the preceeding decades, finally erupted into all-out war. The armies of the Austro-Hungarian Empire and of Germany on the one side, were ranged against the forces of France and Russia on the other. All these countries were in a state of mobilisation at the beginning of August. Britain was drawn into the war when Germany invaded Belgium, a country whose neutrality Britain had promised to protect.

The war lasted for four years and involved 28 countries. It was fought on land and sea and in the air, using the new technology of the aeroplane, the tank and the submarine. It also involved cavalry troops, millions of foot soldiers, loaded wagons drawn by mules, and long months of stubborn resistance and fruitless death in the trenches. In the Battle of the Somme from June to November 1916, the British and German sides lost 500,000 men each; the French, 200,000. By the time the Armistice was signed on November 11th, 1918, nine million soldiers and thirteen million civilians had died, with thirteen million wounded: the greatest slaughter ever recorded in history.

In Britain, the war touched everyone's lives, not through civilian bombing, though that occurred on a limited scale, but through conscription - of men into the armed forces and of women into industry. The army was drawn at first from volunteeers, most of whom expected to be home again within months. As they died in their thousands and the war did not end, compulsory military service was introduced for the first time in Britain in May 1916.

From the Isle of Dogs hundreds of boys still in their teens, as well as older men, went away to war. The Roll of Honour of the Parish of St. Luke's records the names of 685 who served, 115 of whom were killed. If each of the Island's three parishes were represented to the same degree, that would add up to over 2,000 soldiers and sailors, with a loss of well over 300 lives. Potentially up to one-tenth of the Island's total population was therefore removed, and the majority of them were wage-earners. Amongst those who returned were a number who could no longer work as a result of war wounds and shell shock.

One of those who volunteered at 17 and who was discharged when too severely wounded to fight any longer, was Albert Conn of Cuba Street. His experiences impressed him deeply and in later life he wrote down for his descendants some of his memories of trench warfare. The edited version of Albert's recollections, which follows, can stand for the many who trod in the same grisly tracks of war.

"When I was young I lived among smells. The smell of the river Thames. The black scummy water that swished around the rotted piers of the old riverside wharves had a smell of its own, carrying the flotsam backwards and forwards with the tide - rotten fruit, dead bloated cats and dogs. Hungry grey screaming gulls dived and fought for the scraps of food thrown from the galleys of the rusty old tramps moored to the buoys in mid-stream. The scream of the winches and the smell of tarry rope; the old wooden barges bobbed and groaned at their moorings; sunset, and the dirty water turned to cloth of gold. Lights of green, gold and red sprang to life in the night, shimmering and scintillating reflections in the water below. Deep mournful hoots penetrated our stuffy little bedroom through the yellow fog. Street lamps were islands of light shining on the cobbles. The smell of the street. Dried horse dung, twittering sparrows; the sweet smell of beer and the sickly smell of bugs. The smell of perspiration.

My Mother. Red swollen arms in the washtub. My mother was a wonderful woman, looked after our large family like a broody hen and her family of chicks. Sometimes she would have a little cry - we were often short of money. All our groceries were on tick, I used to pop round the corner with little notes to the grocer. I can smell that shop now, broken biscuits and corned beef and the bell that jangled when you pushed the old door open.

Pawning a suit or blankets and sheets now and again. I used to go down to the pawnbrokers, I can see the old three brass balls and still smell the musty back room where the pledges were kept.

The street had a life of its own. Barrel organs and street hawkers, oranges four a penny, barrows piled high, shell fish, baked potatoes, the lavender girl, they all went up and down the street, trundling their wares over the cobbles, each had his or her own peculiar call.

Everybody knew everybody's business. We all knew when Flo or Maggie was pregnant long before it began to show. It was like a jungle telephone, it went from door to door. If you were ever fortunate enough to have any new clothes on all the old women stood at the doors to watch you go by. Skinny dogs sniffed at the old lampposts and stray cats dived into the dirty dustbins searching for the bones of bloater or kipper. People never rushed about in a hurry. The old women sat on their window sills nattering for hours.

There was an old one-horse bus too. It used to run at certain times from the Dock House to Charlie Brown's. Old Charlie Brown used to drive up Westcombe Hill on a Sunday morning in an open trap with a big carriage dog trotting behind. Charlie Brown's, that was the place for prostitutes, every now and again the police would round them up and in the van they would go, swearing and cursing. Limehouse was full of Chinamen, they all wore their pigtails in those days. Puck a Poo was all the rage.

I loved colours; the reflection of a patch of blue sky in a puddle of dirty water would turn it into a thing of beauty for me. I longed to draw and paint, it was the only thing I was fairly good at. But there was no encouragement for that kind of thing in those days. So when I was old enough to leave school I fell in line with the rest and after one or two little jobs I settled for a clerical job with a firm of paint manufacturers on the riverside.

Then came the war. War was declared in August 1914. It turned everything upside down.

War is a terrible thing. I suppose there will always be wars. People never learn. Not that I think there is any glory in it, believe me, there is none. I don't want anybody to get the impression that I was brave - far from it. I was a volunteer, right enough, but that was when I did not know any better. As the war went on, I was scared. Don't make any mistake about that. I imaged that every shell I heard was going to tear my guts out. The amazing thing was that I managed to conceal my fear. Of course, I was incredibly lucky too.

I was too young to get into the army right away. Most people thought it could not last long, three months or a little longer. But it dragged on and one fine day I decided to try and enlist by putting my age on a year or so.

The obvious place to try was our local recruiting station at Tredegar Road, Bow, the HQ of the 17th Company of the London Regiment, the old Poplar and Stepney Rifles. I passed all right but I think they rumbled my age (I was 17) with the result that I was kept at the Depot. We did our training on Hackney Marshes, we also did a lot of recruiting marches through the City.

After a bit I got fed up with all this and began to think of a way to get out of it. I decided to try and enlist in another regiment. I made a bundle of my uniform and left it at home to be collected by whoever would be sent to collect me, and I went to Francis Street, Woolwich and enlisted in the Devon

Regiment. This move altered the whole course of my life.

I can still feel the wonder of looking out of those windows as the train flashed through the Devon countryside. It was the first time I had ever seen country like this; it was all a great adventure. Exeter was my first stop and after a night or two in barracks I was sent to Devonport. Here I completed my training at Granby and Raglan Barracks.

Training was fairly easy, long route marches on the moors, bayonet fighting and firing on ranges in Cornwall. I enjoyed it all except the stupid saluting and counter marching. I think that if a man is good with a rifle and can disappear into the earth with the aid of an entrenching tool in double quick time then he has a much better chance of survival than a man who is as stiff as a poker and strains the muscles of his arms saluting officers, who nine times out of ten don't understand the men they are supposed to lead into battle.

We weren't soldiers, we were civilians in uniform, each with his own problem - how to survive the duration of the war. Food - well, it could have been improved, but I found that I managed better than some of the lads. Those that came from families that had been well brought up and had never experienced the seamy side of life, found our conditions hard.

I met a young lady while on pass one evening in Devonport. We got to know one another very well. She was a cashier in the local Co-operative Stores. She was clean and smart, had wonderful eyes and hair, and lived in a small, neat little house in Stoke Devonport. She invited me home and I was made very welcome by her parents. She was very good to me in many ways, sending me parcels of food and cigarettes when I eventually went overseas. The time I spent in Devonport will always be one of the happiest of my life.

I finished my training and one day was posted up for draft to France. I had my embarkation leave and went home to the old street for a few days. Khaki was the fashionable colour and I was made a fuss of by my brothers and sisters. My leave passed all too quickly and back I went to Devonport.

I went overseas about the end of 1915. I joined the 8th Battalion Devons, 21st brigade, 7th Division at a small village called Allee-sur-Somme near the city of Amiens. We spent Christmas in this village, moving up the line towards the Somme shortly afterwards.

Albert's sweetheart, Winifred. They met in Plymouth whilst he was training. They corresponded during the war and subsequently married and lived on the Island.

The old drum and fife band beat out the tune of "The Farmer's Boy" as "A" Company, heavily laden with packs and ammunition, made their way through the village on to the straight road leading to Becordal and Fricourt. We were on our way to take over the front line from the Cheshire Regiment. It was my first experience of trench warfare.

It was a severe winter and the snow covered the whole countryside like a white blanket. The bare branches of the trees stood out stark against the grey sky. We passed the cross roads skirting shell-torn Becordal on our left. The hanging Virgin from the tower in the Church at Albert gleamed fitfully in the weak winter sun far away.

We came to a small cemetery at the end of the communication trenches, the small wooden crosses with their artificial wreaths capped with snow. In the distance, the sharp rat-tat of a lone machine gun and the dull thud of an exploding shell. It was fairly quiet as we followed in single file up the the long winding trench of the front line; here we were allocated fire bays. Shedding my pack, I took a look through the box periscope at the barbed wire and the humps of earth and snow marking the German parapet. Strange to think I was here at last.

We settled down to the routine of trench life, manning the fire step at dawn and dusk, filling sandbags and repairing trenches. We were detailed off for wiring parties at night and patrols into no-man's-land.

On our left was a weather-beaten crucifix facing the German parapet, a shallow gap ran out through the barbed wire which we used to get out between the trenches, we called it "Crucifix Corner". It was a rare place for snipers, explosive bullets cracked into the sandbags whenever anybody passed. There was a large board with the words "Duck Your Nut" roughly painted on it.

At times during the day the German artillery would shell us with everything they had, all we could do was to hang on while the tremendous explosions showered us with earth and the cries for stretcher bearers rang out right and left. Our artillery could do nothing in return, they were rationed to a certain number of rounds a day and many of these fell short.

On one occasion at Crucifix Corner when the 2nd Gordons were relieving us, the trench had been blown in by a shell burst, one of the Gordons who was trying to pass me in a hurry with our full packs got entangled with me and a sniper got him in the stomach with an explosive bullet. It was an awful wound. We got him on a waterproof sheet and dragged him clear. The sheet filled up with blood, he muttered a few words, I heard him say "Mother", then he must have died soon afterwards.

We continued to occupy these trenches right through the winter and spring, ten days and nights in and ten days and nights sleeping in the barns and outhouses of Meaulte. For a time we were happy enough to be out of the line, sometimes we were paid, and spent our five francs on eggs and chips cooked in one of the farm houses.

It began to snow a lot in February, the whole area for miles around was covered deeply. No-man's-land was blanketed, the ugly shell holes were obliterated and the frost sparkled on the barbed wire. Very lights lit the place up just like a Christmas card, but death lurked there waiting for anybody foolish enough to admire the scenery.

I spent long nights on sentry alone in the fire bay, straining my eyes peering at the German lines in the distance. I could hear their transport behind the village. The large black rats disturbed the empty bully beef tins out in front of the wire, causing them to tinkle, made my hair stand on end thinking a German patrol was cutting the wire. Every now and again a lone machine gun would traverse the parapet and then I would hear a soft ploo from the trenches and watch an object like a comet coming our way.

These mortars, which we named "Flying Pigs" caused havoc if they fell in a fire bay. We used to get hot stew about mid-day, a large dixie would be carried by two men with a pick handle passed through the handles, along the front line. We would have our canteens ready, they would drop the dixie and serve the men in the fire bay and then move on. They had served us one day and went on towards Crucifix Corner when a mortar dropped right in the trench, killing them and scattering their remains and stew in all directions.

We suffered terribly from the cold, there were no shelters or dug-outs in the front line and we were forbidden to light fires. I saw little spirals of smoke from the German parapet where they were cooking.

We were lousy too, everybody was lousy, in the hair on your chest and under your armpits. I even found lice in the knot of the string of my identity disc one day. We burnt them out of the seams of our clothes with lighted candles, but they came back. Sometimes we were issued with clean greybacks from the divisional laundry, the eggs were already in the seams.

The weeks passed, the snow melted and the familiar landmarks appeared again. The rains came and the air was warmer. One morning I listened to larks singing high up in the blue sky. Then one summer's day we were relieved and the whole Division marched away to the little villages behind the Somme line. Here we began to train for the big push on the 1st of July. It was good to settle down in these barns and sleep on straw, read a letter from home and maybe open a parcel. We forgot the whiz-bangs and the wooden crosses we had left behind.

Fricourt and Mametz, June 1916: One of our blokes was shot for desertion the other day. They often form us up in a square and the Adjutant reads out the names of the men of various regiments who have been executed for desertion. I think this bloke of ours was suffering from shellshock. They picked him up around Amiens somewhere. He was sitting in a field, picking daisies, they say.

We have lectures on the Glorious Seventh, so I reckon we are about to be sacrificed to the God of War. I am now a member of our Lewis Gun team, Number Three to be exact. My part of the programme is to cart these great buckets of ammo around. I have a couple slung round my neck. In addition I have a spade, rifle and all my battle gear. I feel like a mule. I shall certainly dump some of this rubbish when I get into action. In my opinion the only valuable item is my entrenching tool. This I wear back to front covering my stomach. It could deflect a bullet or a piece of shrapnel.

We were inspected by Haig the other day. A little grey old man on a big black charger. He had an escort of "Death or Glory" boys. Long lances with pennants flying. I reckon he thinks he is back in the Boer War. What a swindle this war is! The people back home don't know what's going on. What's the good of moaning? It won't get you anywhere Survive! That's the idea. Dig as fast as you can and hope for the best. We shall soon be leaving this haven of rest and I'm not looking forward to it.

Ypres 1916: Fred was a decent sort of bloke. He was much older than me, old enough to be my father. I never knew anything about his folks, whether he was married or single. I don't think he got much mail from home. I got a fair amount, mostly from my girl in Devonport. Every now and again there was a parcel with some Woodbines and a cake I used to share with Fred, sort of mucking-in pals, we were. I remember I had a rubber pillow from her on one occasion, the sort of thing you blow up and rest your head on at night, we finished up playing football with it in a French farmhouse. One time there was a tin of Harrison's Pomade, it was a kind of Vaseline but smelt terrible, it was supposed to kill the lice, I think they thrived on it, I had the biggest and fattest lice in the company.

Fred joined us from the base after we got cut up badly at Mametz. He had previously served with the Gloucesters. He still wore his old cap badge. He was Number Four on our gun, I was Number Three. Our job was to cart the ammo about. One day we were resting near Amiens when Fred suggested we should have our photos taken. We went into a house where a Frenchman with an old-fashioned tripod camera underneath a big black cloth took our pictures. A few days afterwards we marched back to the Somme. We were occupying an old German trench when we got orders to move out that night.

We were checking weapons and ammo when the mail came up. I had a box of fags, proper posh ones they were, called High Life, gold-tipped too. I shared them with Fred just as darkness was settling in. It was a bad night, rain coming down in sheets. In the distance the sky was flickering with flares and gun fire, we could hear the thudding of the bombardment. We struggled along with these panniards slung around our shoulders, rifle, ammo and spade as well as the rest of the fighting order, I always reckoned a bloke was half dead before he ever reached the enemy. Our officer seemed to lose his way several times. Once we found ourselves in Trones Wood. They must have had a hell of a bust-up here. The trees were just stumps sticking out of the ground and the place stank of dead bodies.

Well, we got on eventually and found the rest of the lads in an old communication trench near Guillemont. This village had been taken and retaken several times. For some unknown reason the Germans were loath to part with it. By the sound of the bombardment I shouldn't think there could have been anything left.

There was a steady stream of wounded making their way towards the dressing station and we asked one or two what it was like in front of the village. They said the bombardment was terrible, so you can bet we didn't feel too happy. It was still raining so I tried to get a bit of a kip before dawn, in those days I could sleep on a clothes line. I pulled my waterproof cape over my head and settled down in the mud. I was jolted out of my sleep by a sharp blow on the inside of my right knee. I thought somebody must have kicked me. Half asleep, I felt my leg and my hand came away wet and sticky.

I thought to myself, Blimey, I've got a Blighty one. It was deep and about a couple of inches long. Fred tied a field bandage on it. He then helped me down the trench and out onto the road. The first dressing station was down a mile of steps and the Officer refused to dress my wound because I did not belong to his Division. We found another one further down the road and here I shook hands with Fred. He wished me luck and said that should I reach Blighty would I contact his people in Bristol, I promised to do so, but strangely enough he never

A list of some of the books and articles consulted or referred to in the text.

About the East End

Burrell and Company, *A Century in Colour*, pub. by the firm in 1952

Cole, Tom, *Life and Labour in the Isle of Dogs: the origins and evolution of an East London working-class community*, unpublished PhD thesis. University of Oklahoma, 1981

Cowper, Benjamin H., *A Descriptive, Historical and Statistical Account of Millwall, Commonly called the Isle of Dogs*, Gladding, 1853.

Free, Richard, *Seven Years Hard*, Heinemann, 1904

Ellmers, Chris, and others, *London's Riverscape Lost and Found*, London, Checkmate/Art Books International, 2000

George, Millicent, *London Life in the Eighteenth Century*, Kegan Paul, 1930

Gomme G.L. *New Subway for Foot Passengers between Millwall and Greenwich* London County Council, 1902

Hawkins, C., *The Story of Hawkins & Tipson, Ropemakers*, pub. by the company, 1952

McDonnell, Kevin, *Medieval London Suburbs*, Phillimore, 1978

McDonnell, Kevin, *The Economic and Social Structure of the parishes of Bromley, Hackney, Stepney and Whitechapel from the 13th to the 16th centuries*, unpublished PhD. thesis, 1959.

McDougall's Ltd., *A Matter of History, A Century of McDougall's Self Raising Flour*, 1964

Mayhew, Henry, *London Labour and the London Poor*, Dover Publications, 1968

Palmer, Alan, *The East End: Four Centuries of London Life*, Murray, London 2000

Pollard, Sydney, *The Decline of Shipbuilding on the Thames*, in The Economic History Review, 1950.

Porter, Stephen (ed), *Survey of London, Vols. XLIII and XLIV, Poplar, Blackwall and the Isle of Dogs, The Parish of All Saints*, Athlone Press, 1994.

Pudney, John, *London's Docks*, Thames & Hudson, London, 1975

Thompson, Paul, *Socialists, Liberals and Labour: The Struggle for London 1885-1914*, RKP 1967

Wright, Thomas, *Some Habits and Customs of the Working Classes, by A Journeyman Engineer*, 1867

General Reading

Burnett, John, *A Social History of Housing 1815-1970*, Methuen, 1978

Checkland, S.G., *The Rise of Industrial Society in England, 1815-1885*, Longman, 1964

Dyos H.J. & Aldcroft, D.H. *British Transport: An Economic Survey from the 17th century to the 20th*, Penguin, 1974

Holmes, G. (ed.), *The Oxford History of Medieval Europe*. OUP, 1988

Hill, C., *Reformation to Industrial Revolution*, Penguin, 1976

Hill, C.P., *British Economic and Social History 1700-1939*, Arnold, 1967

Le Goff, J. (ed.), *The Medieval World*, Parkgate Books, 1997

Meacham, Standish, *A Life Apart, The English Working Class 1890-1914*, Thames and Hudson, 1977

Morton, A.L., *A People's History of England*, Lawrence & Wishart, 1979

Morton, A., and Tate, G., *The British Labour Movement*, Lawrence and Wishart, 1979

Plumb, J.H., *England in the Eighteenth Century*, Penguin, 1968

Thomas, K., *Religion and the Decline of Magic*, Penguin, 1973